NORTHROP GRUMMAN CORPORATION

USS Forrest Sherman

AUTHOR'S NOTES

For over 25 years Maritime Books has produced *British Warships and Auxiliaries*, an annual guide to the ships, aircraft and weapons of the Royal Navy. Always eagerly awaited, the handy pocket-sized format of the book has found favour amongst, not only those with a professional interest in the Royal Navy, but also those keen amateurs who spend hours around the UK Naval Bases photographing warships as they arrive or depart, and even those, who may have but a passing interest, but are keen to find out a little more about the ships they see around the coast and have paid for as taxpayers.

Always keen to receive feedback, we have, over the years, had a recurring theme to such correspondence - *"When are you going to do a book on the US Navy?"*

In the past, I have always dismissed such a project. The book is intended to be a handy reference, readily available, whether that be in your pocket, car, or camera bag - How could I condense a volume on the US Navy into such a compact formula?

Well, having bitten the bullet, and deciding to take the project on, the finished volume still retains the flavour of the original - a picture entry for each class, together with brief technical information and a short background paragraph - without being too big so as not to fit in your pocket!

Reasearching such a vast topic as this is never easy, and though both the USN and Military Sealift Command have extensive and informative websites, the information contained on them can only be as current as the last update. In trying to iron out some of the conflicting information I have been most fortunate to have had the seemingly endless help and support from numerous USN, MSC and MARAD Public Affairs Offices, for whom, it would seem, no request is too difficult (or in some cases obscure!). My thanks, in particular, must go to Laura Seal (Military Sealift Command) and Susan Clark (MARAD) who helped with information and images on the more elusive vessels of the MSC and Ready Reserve Fleet

I must also acknowledge the help of George Del Gaudio of Orange County, California. Having met him in San Diego in June 2006, I chanced to send him an e-mail seeking clarification on a decommissioning date - since which time e-mails and letters providing constant updates, have been pouring in!

I must also acknowledge the work of the photographers of both the military and naval shipbuilders. It would appear that weather and sea state are not a deterrent to these professional photographers who strive to capture the true power of these vessels in their natural environment - the distant ocean. I have drawn extensively on their images, without which this volume would be a dry list of technical information. Where known, individuals are credited alongside each image.

This book can only be as up to date as the day it was printed, but any errors which may have crept in are solely my own, and I would be grateful to be made aware of any so that they can be updated in any future editions. Contact me at warshipworld@navy-books.com

Steve Bush
Cornwall, December 2006

THE UNITED STATES NAVY

There can be little doubt, that the US Navy of today is the most powerful fleet in the world. Although at just shy of 300 ships, a mere shadow of its former 'Cold War' 600 ship navy, the USN still comfortably maintains a global presence. Centred around fleets in the Atlantic (2nd Fleet), Pacific (3rd and 7th Fleets), the Gulf (5th Fleet) and Europe (6th Fleet), the USN has a massive global footprint.

Since the end of the Cold War, the USN has slowly been evolving into an expeditionary force, being more flexible in its operating patterns and able to deploy varied assets at short notice, in response to world crises.

This is being achieved through the Fleet Response Plan (FRP). This changes the way ships are maintained, and keeps the Navy at a high state of readiness, providing the capability of deploying a number of Carrier Strike Groups (CSGs), in whole or part, immediately to wherever in the world the mission calls, with additional CSGs deploying within 90 days of the request to do so. Under current plans six CSGs could be ready to deploy within 30 days of notification and another within 90 days. The FRP concept was vividly demonstrated by the response to Hurricane Katrina, in which 23 ships were immediately made available for relief efforts.

AIRCRAFT CARRIERS

Central to the USNs strike capability is the aircraft carrier which operate in CSGs, which usually comprise, in addition to the carrier, a cruiser, two destroyers, an attack submarine and a supply vessel. The USN presently has 11 aircraft carriers. By 2008, when KITTY HAWK retires, all will be nuclear-powered. The oldest, ENTERPRISE, was completed in 1961 and by the time she is scheduled to decommission in 2013 she will be 52 years old - certainly value for money! The last of the Nimitz class carriers is scheduled to complete in 2008, and the next generation of carriers, the CVN 21 class are scheduled to begin construction shortly.

AMPHIBIOUS FORCES

The CSGs are backed up by a massive amphibious force. Traditionally these deployed as Amphibious Ready Groups (ARG), centred around a 'flat-top' amphib (LHA or LHD) and usually a part of a CVBG. Now these too deploy as Expeditionary Strike Groups (ESG), again centred around an LHA or LHD, but with their own escort group, enabling them to act independently of the CSG.

The USN has ten LHA/LHD, with MAKIN ISLAND scheduled to commission in 2007. A new LHA(R) building programme is underway to replace the older Tarawa class ships.

The 30 year old Austin class LPDs are being repaced by the new state of the art San Antonio class nine of which are in build or on order.

There are 12 Landing Ship Docks, each capable of operating helicopters and Landing Craft Air Cushion (LCAC) to deliver troops and stores ashore.

The Amphibious assets are backed up by a massive fleet of pre-positioned ships, located at strategic locations around the world. These vessels remain fully stored and equipped with the vehicles, ammunition and heavy equipment required by an expeditionary fighting force. The limitations of these vessels has now been recognised, in as much as they can deliver their cargo, but then become very much surplus to requirements.

The Future Maritime Pre-positioning Force MPF(F) is in the planning stage and the sea basing concept is being studied. The concept is to set up a large operating base in a forward area (25-100 miles off shore from the target destination) This base could consist of MPF vessels, auxiliaries and amphibious vessels. The MPF ships will be larger than present ships and have facilities to accept troops aboard at sea, accommodate them and marry them up to their equipment. The ships would also have aviation facilities and ramps allowing transfer of troops and equipment by helicopter and LCAC. In addition they could provide command and control, medical and resupply facilities, thereby regenerating the frontline, without having to leave the area. It is possible that between 12-18 such vessels of 70-90,000 tons could be acquired by 2009.

SUBMARINES

The USN operates the sea-based leg of the nuclear deterrent with a fleet of 14 Ohio class submarines, each armed with 24 Trident ICBMs. Although there are no plans to replace these submarines in the immediate future, funds have been allocated to a missile life extension programme.

Four former Trident submarines have completed conversion into potent land attack submarines. With the Trident system removed, the four submarines can deliver up to 154 Tomahawk missiles each, in addition to accommodating and deploying special forces.

The Los Angeles attack submarine programme was completed in 1996 and the Virginia class are beginning to enter service. It is planned to be a class of 30 submarines and the build tempo is likely to be 1-2 vessels a year. With the oldest Los Angeles class already 30 years old, it is likely that the total number of attack submarines numbers will reduce before all of the Virginia class enter service.

ESCORTS

USN escorts have tended to be categorised by role, rather than size, with cruisers taking on air defence, destroyers anti-surface and frigates anti-submarine warfare. The Ticonderoga class cruisers are expected to serve for at least 35 years (the oldest in service in 2007, BUNKER HILL, commissioned in 1986 and the newest, PORT ROYAL, in 1994). All are expected to undergo a mid-life extension work package. The Arleigh Burke class continue in production (62 ships envisaged) and are very capable ships, able to take on air defence, in addition to anti-ship duties. Several of these destroyers (and Ticonderoga class) have been converted to take on the Anti-ballistic missile role, centring around an upgraded Aegis system coupled with the SM-3 missile.

Only 30 of the original 51 FFG 7 class frigates remain in USN service, the ASW role having taken a bit of a back seat since the end of the Cold War. Those ships remaining in service have had their Mk13 missile launcher removed, thereby reducing the effectiveness of these ships as fleet assets.

MINOR WAR VESSELS

The USN has had a love hate relationship with small warships. Today there are three classes of small warship in service - two of mine countermeasures vessels and one of patrol craft.

The USN seabased MCM force was regenerated in the 1980s when it acquired 14 Avenger class ocean-going minehunters and 12 Osprey class Coastal minehunters. It would appear that the honeymoon period is over, with the entire Osprey class due to decommission by 2008. It is true that much of their capabilities will be taken up by the new LCS (see Future Fleet) and in part by self contained MCM gear fitted to some destroyers, but after years of neglecting this capability it seems strange that it has fallen by the wayside so quickly - again.

The Cyclone class Patrol Craft of the USN have always seemed to be a ship looking for a role. Unsuited to their initial role of special forces ships, they have been held variously in lay-up, seconded to the US Coast Guard and at times operated on interdiction operations in the Caribbean and on homeland security duties post 9/11.

The Global War on Terror however, seems to have given these ships a new lease of life. They appear to be ideally suited to operations in the Persian Gulf and between 2 and 4 ships have been detached to that area of operations for shallow water patrols, security and interdiction operations.

FUTURE FLEET

Some of the new shipbuilding programmes have already been mentioned, CVN 21, LHA(R), San Antonio class, Virginia Class and the ongoing Arleigh Burke programme. In addition there are several classes of new, innovative designs, either on the drawing board, or under construction.

Future shipbuilding plans call for a Surface Combatant "Family of Ships": In addition to the USN's next-generation destroyer (DDG 1000 or Zumwalt class) and cruiser, CG(X), the Surface Combatant Family of Ships concept calls for the introduction of a new Littoral Combat Ship (LCS). This vessel has been described as a small, fast, maneouverable, and relatively inexpensive member of the Surface Combatant Family of Ships, which began construction in 2005. The goal is to develop a vessel that can be fielded in relatively large numbers to support a wide range of joint missions, through the use of modular mission modules, to allow access to coastal waters, while combatting threats from surface craft, submarines, and mines.

The Zumwalt class, next generation destroyer, will be a multi-mission ship with enhanced precision strike capability and and the ability to provide high volume naval gunfire support and missile strike against land targets. DDG-1000 ZUMWALT will be the lead ship. The class received Milestone B approval on 23 November 2005 , clearing the way for the Navy to commence detail design and construction.

CG(X) will be a multi-mission ship follow-on to DDG-1000 with enhanced Missile Defence and Air Warfare capability. The CG(X) cruiser will replace the Ticonderoga class AEGIS cruisers. Providing an 'umbrella' of air and missile defence, with longer-range missiles, the ships will be able to protect Carrier Strike Groups and other vessels. It will also be able to track and engage ballistic missiles hundreds of miles inland. Currently the CG(X) is in the design phase.

CONCLUSION

The United States Navy has, since the end of the Cold War, transitioned from a blue water leviathan prepared for a super-power to super-power conflict, into a flexible and very powerful expeditionary strike force capable of rapid deployment and able to deliver previously unheard of firepower from sea to shore.

It is equipping itself and training for warfare in the restricted littoral waters where future naval forces are expected to operate. New warships are being developed and built and new tactics being developed. Traditional deep water anti-submarine warfare doesn't work in the cluttered coastal waters, so the USN has leased a state of the art diesel powered submarine from the Swedish Navy in 2004. Typical of the submarines to be found in such waters the USN is using it to retrain its sonar operators in the art of coastal ASW.

If all future shipbuilding plans come to fruition, the USN will be able to conduct operations offshore, and in the littorals, supported and sustained by purpose built vessels operating as mobile sea bases. Fully independent of shore bases for resupply or air operations, the USN will be able to strike from the sea, below the sea and above the sea; return to bases at sea and withdraw on completion - by sea. A truly formidable example of expeditionary warfare.

SHIPS OF THE UNITED STATES NAVY
Pennant Numbers

Ship	Pennant Number	Ship	Pennant Number
Aircraft Carriers		HOUSTON	SSN 713
		NORFOLK	SSN 714
KITTY HAWK	CV 63	BUFFALO	SSN 715
ENTERPRISE	CVN 65	OLYMPIA	SSN 717
JOHN F. KENNEDY	CV 67	PROVIDENCE	SSN 719
NIMITZ	CVN 68	PITTSBURGH	SSN 720
DWIGHT D. EISENHOWER	CVN 69	CHICAGO	SSN 721
CARL VINSON	CVN 70	KEY WEST	SSN 722
THEODORE ROOSEVELT	CVN 71	OKLAHOMA CITY	SSN 723
ABRAHAM LINCOLN	CVN 72	LOUISVILLE	SSN 724
GEORGE WASHINGTON	CVN 73	HELENA	SSN 725
JOHN C. STENNIS	CVN 74	OHIO	SSGN 726
HARRY S. TRUMMAN	CVN 75	MICHIGAN	SSGN 727
RONALD REAGAN	CVN 76	FLORIDA	SSGN 728
GEORGE H.W. BUSH	CVN 77	GEORGIA	SSGN 729
		HENRY M. JACKSON	SSBN 730
Submarines		ALABAMA	SSBN 731
		ALASKA	SSBN 732
SEAWOLF	SSN 21	NEVADA	SSBN 733
CONNECTICUT	SSN 22	TENNESSEE	SSBN 734
JIMMY CARTER	SSN 23	PENNSYLVANIA	SSBN 735
LOS ANGELES	SSN 688	WEST VIRGINIA	SSBN 736
PHILADELPHIA	SSN 690	KENTUCKY	SSBN 737
MEMPHIS	SSN 691	MARYLAND	SSBN 738
BREMERTON	SSN 698	NEBRASKA	SSBN 739
JACKSONVILLE	SSN 699	RHODE ISLAND	SSBN 740
DALLAS	SSN700	MAINE	SSBN 741
LA JOLLA	SSN 701	WYOMING	SSBN 742
CITY OF CORPUS CHRISTI	SSN 705	LOUISIANA	SSBN 743
ALBUQUERQUE	SSN 706	NEWPORT NEWS	SSN 750
MINNEAPOLIS-ST. PAUL	SSN 708	SAN JUAN	SSN 751
HYMAN G. RICKOVER	SSN 709	PASADENA	SSN 752
AUGUSTA	SSN 710	ALBANY	SSN 753
SAN FRANCISCO	SSN 711	TOPEKA	SSN 754

Ship	Pennant Number	Ship	Pennant Number
MIAMI	SSN 755	PRINCETON	CG 59
SCRANTON	SSN 756	NORMANDY	CG 60
ALEXANDRIA	SSN 757	MONTEREY	CG 61
ASHEVILLE	SSN 758	CHANCELLORSVILLE	CG 62
JEFFERSON CITY	SSN 759	COWPENS	CG 63
ANNAPOLIS	SSN 760	GETTYSBURG	CG 64
SPRINGFIELD	SSN 761	CHOSIN	CG 65
COLUMBUS	SSN 762	HUE CITY	CG 66
SANTA FE	SSN 763	SHILOH	CG 67
BOISE	SSN 764	ANZIO	CG 68
MONTPELIER	SSN 765	VICKSBURG	CG 69
CHARLOTTE	SSN 766	LAKE ERIE	CG 70
HAMPTON	SSN 767	CAPE ST. GEORGE	CG 71
HARTFORD	SSN 768	VELLA GULF	CG 72
TOLEDO	SSN 769	PORT ROYAL	CG 73
TUCSON	SSN 770		
COLUMBIA	SSN 771	**Destroyers**	
GREENEVILLE	SSN 772		
CHEYENNE	SSN 773	ARLEIGH BURKE	DDG 51
VIRGINIA	SSN 774	BARRY	DDG 52
TEXAS	SSN 775	JOHN PAUL JONES	DDG 53
HAWAII	SSN 776	CURTIS WILBUR	DDG 54
NORTH CAROLINA	SSN 777	STOUT	DDG 55
NEW HAMPSHIRE	SSN 778	JOHN S. McCAIN	DDG 56
NEW MEXICO	SSN 779	MITSCHER	DDG 57
NOT YET NAMED	SSN 780	LABOON	DDG 58
NOT YET NAMED	SSN 781	RUSSELL	DDG 59
		PAUL HAMILTON	DDG 60
		RAMAGE	DDG 61
Cruisers		FITZGERALD	DDG 62
		STETHEM	DDG 63
BUNKER HILL	CG 52	CARNEY	DDG 64
MOBILE BAY	CG 53	BENFOLD	DDG 65
ANTIETAM	CG 54	GONZALEZ	DDG 66
LEYTE GULF	CG 55	COLE	DDG 67
SAN JACINTO	CG 56	THE SULLIVANS	DDG 68
LAKE CHAMPLAIN	CG 57	MILIUS	DDG 69
PHILIPPINE SEA	CG 58	HOPPER	DDG 70

Ship	Pennant Number	Ship	Pennant Number
ROSS	DDG 71	*NOT YET NAMED*	DDG 109
MAHAN	DDG 72	*NOT YET NAMED*	DDG 110
DECATUR	DDG 73	*NOT YET NAMED*	DDG 111
McFAUL	DDG 74	*NOT YET NAMED*	DDG 112
DONALD COOK	DDG 75		
HIGGINS	DDG 76	**Frigates**	
O'KANE	DDG 77		
PORTER	DDG 78	McINERNEY	FFG 8
OSCAR AUSTIN	DDG 79	BOONE	FFG 28
ROOSEVELT	DDG 80	STEPHEN W. GROVES	FFG 29
WINSTON S. CHURCHILL	DDG 81	JOHN L. HALL	FFG 32
LASSEN	DDG 82	JARRETT	FFG 33
HOWARD	DDG 83	UNDERWOOD	FFG 36
BULKELEY	DDG 84	CROMMELIN	FFG 37
McCAMPBELL	DDG 85	CURTS	FFG 38
SHOUP	DDG 86	DOYLE	FFG 39
MASON	DDG 87	HALYBURTON	FFG 40
PREBLE	DDG 88	McCLUSKY	FFG 41
MUSTIN	DDG 89	KLAKRING	FFG 42
CHAFEE	DDG 90	THACH	FFG 43
PINCKNEY	DDG 91	DE WERT	FFG 45
MOMSEN	DDG 92	RENTZ	FFG 46
CHUNG-HOON	DDG 93	NICHOLAS	FFG 47
NITZE	DDG 94	VANDEGRIFT	FFG 48
JAMES E. WILLIAMS	DDG 95	ROBERT G. BRADLEY	FFG 49
BAINBRIDGE	DDG 96	TAYLOR	FFG 50
HALSEY	DDG 97	GARY	FFG 51
FORREST SHERMAN	DDG 98	CARR	FFG 52
FARRAGUT	DDG 99	HAWES	FFG 53
KIDD	DDG 100	FORD	FFG 54
GRIDLEY	DDG 101	ELROD	FFG 55
SAMPSON	DDG 102	SIMPSON	FFG 56
TRUXTUN	DDG 103	REUBEN JAMES	FFG 57
STERRETT	DDG 104	SAMUEL B. ROBERTS	FFG 58
DEWEY	DDG 105	KAUFFMAN	FFG 59
STOCKDALE	DDG 106	RODNEY M. DAVIS	FFG 60
GRAVELY	DDG 107	INGRAHAM	FFG 61
NOT YET NAMED	DDG 108		

Ship	Pennant Number	Ship	Pennant Number
Littoral Combat Ships		SAN DIEGO	LPD 22
		ANCHORAGE	LPD 23
FREEDOM	LCS 1	ARLINGTON	LPD 24
INDEPENDENCE	LCS 2	SOMERSET	LPD 25
NOT YET NAMED	LCS 3	WHIDBEY ISLAND	LSD 41
NOT YET NAMED	LCS 4	GERMANTOWN	LSD 42
		FORT McHENRY	LSD 43
		GUNSTON HALL	LSD 44
Amphibious Ships		COMSTOCK	LSD 45
		TORTUGA	LSD 46
BLUE RIDGE	LCC 19	RUSHMORE	LSD 47
MOUNT WHITNEY	LCC 20	ASHLAND	LSD 48
TARAWA	LHA 1	HARPERS FERRY	LSD 49
SAIPAN	LHA 2	CARTER HALL	LSD 50
NASSAU	LHA 4	OAK HILL	LSD 51
PELELIU	LHA 5	PEARL HARBOR	LSD 52
WASP	LHD 1		
ESSEX	LHD 2	**Mine Countermeasures**	
KEARSARGE	LHD 3	**Vessels**	
BOXER	LHD 4		
BATAAN	LHD 5	AVENGER	MCM 1
BONHOMME RICHARD	LHD 6	DEFENDER	MCM 2
IWO JIMA	LHD 7	SENTRY	MCM 3
MAKIN ISLAND	LHD 8	CHAMPION	MCM 4
AUSTIN	LPD 4	GUARDIAN	MCM 5
OGDEN	LPD 5	DEVASTATOR	MCM 6
CLEVELAND	LPD 7	PATRIOT	MCM 7
DUBUQUE	LPD 8	SCOUT	MCM 8
DENVER	LPD 9	PIONEER	MCM 9
JUNEAU	LPD 10	WARRIOR	MCM 10
SHREVEPORT	LPD 12	GLADIATOR	MCM 11
NASHVILLE	LPD 13	ARDENT	MCM 12
TRENTON	LPD 14	DEXTROUS	MCM 13
PONCE	LPD 15	CHIEF	MCM 14
SAN ANTONIO	LPD 17	HERON	MHC 52
NEW ORLEANS	LPD 18	PELICAN	MHC 53
MESA VERDE	LPD 19	KINGFISHER	MHC 56
GREEN BAY	LPD 20	CORMORANT	MHC 57
NEW YORK	LPD 21	BLACK HAWK	MHC 58

Ship	Pennant Number	Ship	Pennant Number
CARDINAL	MHC 60	**Submarine Tenders**	
RAVEN	MHC 61		
SHRIKE	MHC 62	EMORY S. LAND	AS 39
		FRANK CABLE	AS 40
Patrol Craft			
		High Speed Vessel	
HURRICANE	PC 3		
TYPHOON	PC 5	SWIFT	HSV 2
SIROCCO	PC 6		
SQUALL	PC 7	**Miscellaneous Vessels**	
CHINOOK	PC 9		
FIREBOLT	PC 10	DOLPHIN	SS 555
WHIRLWIND	PC 11	NR-1	
THUNDERBOLT	PC 12	SEA FIGHTER	FSF 1
		SEA SHADOW	IX 529
Rescue and Salvage Ship		MYSTIC	DSRV 1
		AVALON	DSRV 2
SAFEGUARD	ARS 50		

USS Pennsylvania

OHIO CLASS SSBN

Ship	Pennant Number	Completion Date	Builder
HENRY M. JACKSON	730	1984	GD (Electric Boat Div)
ALABAMA	731	1985	GD (Electric Boat Div)
ALASKA	732	1986	GD (Electric Boat Div)
NEVADA	733	1986	GD (Electric Boat Div)
TENNESSEE	734	1988	GD (Electric Boat Div)
PENNSYLVANIA	735	1989	GD (Electric Boat Div)
WEST VIRGINIA	736	1990	GD (Electric Boat Div)
KENTUCKY	737	1991	GD (Electric Boat Div)
MARYLAND	738	1992	GD (Electric Boat Div)
NEBRASKA	739	1993	GD (Electric Boat Div)
RHODE ISLAND	740	1994	GD (Electric Boat Div)
MAINE	741	1995	GD (Electric Boat Div)
WYOMING	742	1996	GD (Electric Boat Div)
LOUISIANA	743	1997	GD (Electric Boat Div)

Machinery One nuclear reactor, one shaft **Displacement** 18,750 tons (dived) **Dimensions** 170.7m x 12.8m x 11.1m **Speed** 25 + dived **Armament** 24 - Trident 2 (D5) missiles, 4 Torpedo Tubes **Complement** 155

Notes

These submarine maintain the sea-based leg of the US Nuclear Deterrent Forces, with normally five submarines on station at any one time, five in transit - but still capable of launching missiles, with the remainder in port or overhaul. All 18 of the Ohio-class SSBNs have been commissioned; the final ship of the class, the USS LOUISANA, joined the fleet in 1997. In 2000, the last four of the original eight submarines began conversion to carry the Trident II/D5 missile. USS ALABAMA is the last ship to undergo D5 conversion which began in 2006.

The Trident II/D5 is the sixth generation of the Navy's Fleet Ballistic Missile programme, which started in 1955. The D5 is a three-stage, solid propellant, inertial-guided submarine-launched ballistic missile (SLBM) with a range greater than 4,000 nautical miles and accuracy measured in hundreds of feet. The missiles are capable of carrying W76 or W88 Multiple Independently Targeted Re-entry Vehicles (MIRVs). In operation, Trident II/D5 missiles have been declared at eight MIRV warheads under the Strategic Arms Reduction Treaty. In 2007 funding will be dedicated to the D5 life extension programme. Full missile procurement is to begin in 2008 ending in 2012 with a total acquisition of 108 additional missiles.

Two older Lafayette class SSBNs, DANIEL WEBSTER and SAM RAYBURN remain at Charleston as training vessels for nuclear power systems, though their missile compartments have been removed.

Notes on Decommissioning

By law US nuclear-powered vessels must have crews onboard until their reactors have been defuelled. Therefore, when USN submarines are withdrawn from service they are placed "In Commission, In Reserve." Once defuelled and de-equipped they can be decommissioned and removed (stricken) from the Navy Register. Vessels "In Commission, In Reserve" cannot be recalled to active duty.

USS Florida

OHIO CLASS SSGN

Ship	Pennant Number	Completion Date	Builder
OHIO	726	1981	GD (Electric Boat Div)
MICHIGAN	727	1982	GD (Electric Boat Div)
FLORIDA	728	1983	GD (Electric Boat Div)
GEORGIA	729	1984	GD (Electric Boat Div)

Machinery One nuclear reactor, one shaft **Displacement** 18,750 tons (dived) **Dimensions** 170.7m x 12.8m x 11.1m **Speed** 20 + dived **Armament** Up to 154 Tomahawk missiles, 4 Torpedo Tubes **Complement** 169

Notes

These former Trident submarines were scheduled to be withdrawn from service in 2003/04, however it was decided to convert them to a land attack role. Armed with the Tomahawk missile system, they are also able to carry and support a team of 66 special forces personnel for up to 90 days and insert and retrieve them clandestinely. OHIO commenced her conversion in November 2003; FLORIDA April 2004; MICHIGAN October 2004 and GEORGIA October 2005. On 14 January 2003, FLORIDA became the first Ohio-class submarine to launch a cruise missile, during a test firing prior to coversion. OHIO rejoined the fleet in January 2006. The anticipated cost for all four SSGN conversions is approximately $4 billion.

USS Virginia

ATTACK SUBMARINES
VIRGINIA CLASS

Ship	Pennant Number	Completion Date	Builder
VIRGINIA	774	2004	GD (Electric Boat Div)
TEXAS	775	2006	Newport News SB
HAWAII	776	*2007*	GD (Electric Boat Div)
NORTH CAROLINA	777	*2008*	Newport News SB
NEW HAMPSHIRE	778	*2009*	GD (Electric Boat Div)
NEW MEXICO	779	*2010*	Newport News SB
NOT YET NAMED	780	*2011*	GD (Electric Boat Div)
NOT YET NAMED	781	*2012*	Newport News SB

Machinery One nuclear reactor, one shaft **Displacement** 7,800 tons dived **Dimensions** 114.8m x 10.4m x 8m **Speed** 25 knots + dived **Armament** Tomahawk missiles, 12 VLS tubes, Mk48 ADCAP torpedoes, 4 Torpedo Tubes **Complement** 134.

15

Notes

These advanced submarines will be fully configured to conduct mining and mine reconnaissance, Special Operations Forces insertion/extraction, battle group support, intelli-
gence-collection and surveillance missions, sea-control,and land attack. Further, the
Virginia SSNs will be specifically configured to adapt easily to special missions and
emerging requirements.

The first seven submarines, of an anticipated class of 30, are being built under an innovative teaming arrangement between General Dynamics' Electric Boat Corporation (EB)
and Northrop Grumman Newport News (NGNN). Under the teaming arrangement, construction of the ships will be shared by ship section. NGNN is building the bow, stern, sail,
and selected forward sections for each submarine. EB is building the hull sections, the
engine room modules, and the command-and-control system operating spaces. EB will
assemble and deliver the first, third, and fifth ships; NGNN, the second, fourth, and sixth.
Construction of VIRGINIA began in 1998, TEXAS in 1999, HAWAII 2001, NORTH
CAROLINA in 2002, NEW HAMPSHIRE in 2003 and NEW MEXICO in 2004. The as yet
un-named SSN-780 and SSN-781 began construction in 2005 and 2006 respectively.
The tempo of build is expected to increase to two a year from 2009 in order to maintain
submarine force levels.

The single S9G Pressurised Water Reactor is expected to run for 30 years without refuelling. Reportedly as quiet at 25 knots as a Los Angeles class boat at rest.

USS Seawolf

SEAWOLF CLASS

Ship	Pennant Number	Completion Date	Builder
SEAWOLF	21	1997	GD (Electric Boat Div)
CONNECTICUT	22	1998	GD (Electric Boat Div)
JIMMY CARTER	23	2005	GD (Electric Boat Div)

Machinery One nuclear reactor, one shaft **Displacement** 9,284 tons (SSN23 12,353 tons) **Dimensions** 108m x 12m x 11m (SSN23 138.07m x 12.2m) **Speed** 25+ knots **Armament** Tomahawk missiles, Mk48 Torpedoes, 8 torpedo tubes **Complement** 134.

Notes

The US Navy began construction of the Seawolf class in 1989. SSN 23 is longer to incorporate advanced technologies and a capability to transport and deploy special forces. She can accommodate 50 SEALs and their vehicles. SSN 23 will also deploy in the intelligence gathering role previously conducted by the recently retired PARCHE.

USS Key West

LOS ANGELES CLASS

Ship	Pennant Number	Completion Date	Builder
LOS ANGELES	688	1976	Newport News SB
PHILADELPHIA	690	1977	GD (Electric Boat Div)
MEMPHIS	691	1977	Newport News SB
BREMERTON	698	1981	GD (Electric Boat Div)
JACKSONVILLE	699	1981	GD (Electric Boat Div)
DALLAS	700	1981	GD (Electric Boat Div)
LA JOLLA	701	1981	GD (Electric Boat Div)
CITY OF CORPUS CHRISTI	705	1983	GD (Electric Boat Div)
ALBUQUERQUE	706	1983	GD (Electric Boat Div)
MINNEAPOLIS-ST PAUL	708	1984	GD (Electric Boat Div)
HYMAN G. RICKOVER	709	1984	GD (Electric Boat Div)
AUGUSTA	710	1985	GD (Electric Boat Div)
SAN FRANCISCO	711	1981	Newport News SB
HOUSTON	713	1982	Newport News SB

Ship	Pennant Number	Completion Date	Builder
NORFOLK	714	1983	Newport News SB
BUFFALO	715	1983	Newport News SB
OLYMPIA	717	1984	Newport News SB
PROVIDENCE	719	1985	GD (Electric Boat Div)
PITTSBURGH	720	1985	GD (Electric Boat Div)
CHICAGO	721	1986	Newport News SB
KEY WEST	722	1987	Newport News SB
OKLAHOMA CITY	723	1988	Newport News SB
LOUISVILLE	724	1986	GD (Electric Boat Div)
HELENA	725	1987	GD (Electric Boat Div)
NEWPORT NEWS	750	1989	Newport News SB
SAN JUAN	751	1988	GD (Electric Boat Div)
PASADENA	752	1989	GD (Electric Boat Div)
ALBANY	753	1990	Newport News SB
TOPEKA	754	1989	GD (Electric Boat Div)
MIAMI	755	1990	GD (Electric Boat Div)
SCRANTON	756	1991	Newport News SB
ALEXANDRIA	757	1991	GD (Electric Boat Div)
ASHEVILLE	758	1991	Newport News SB
JEFFERSON CITY	759	1992	Newport News SB
ANNAPOLIS	760	1992	GD (Electric Boat Div)
SPRINGFIELD	761	1993	GD (Electric Boat Div)
COLUMBUS	762	1993	GD (Electric Boat Div)
SANTA FE	7631	1994	GD (Electric Boat Div)
BOISE	764	1992	Newport News SB
MONTPELIER	765	1993	Newport News SB
CHARLOTTE	766	1994	Newport News SB
HAMPTON	767	1993	Newport News SB
HARTFORD	768	1994	GD (Electric Boat Div)

Ship	Pennant Number	Completion Date	Builder
TOLEDO	769	1995	Newport News SB
TUCSON	770	1995	Newport News SB
COLUMBIA	771	1995	GD (Electric Boat Div)
GREENVILLE	772	1996	Newport News SB
CHEYENNE	773	1996	Newport News SB

Machinery One nuclear reactor, one shaft **Displacement** 7,011 tonnes **Dimensions** 110m x 10m x 9.7 **Speed** 20+ knots **Armament** Tomahawk missiles, vertical launch tubes (719 and later) Mk 48 torpedoes, four torpedo tubes **Complement** 140

Notes

Designed as a follow-on to the STURGEON class submarines built during the 1960s, the Los Angeles class incorporated improved sound quietening and a larger propulsion plant than previous classes. Her many capabilities include wartime functions of undersea warfare, surface warfare, strike warfare, mining operations, special forces delivery, reconnaissance, carrier battle group support and escort, and intelligence collection. This large class of submarine evolved during construction and three variants eventually entered service. From PROVIDENCE onwards the submarines were fitted with 12 vertical launch tubes for the Tomahawk cruise missile, along with an upgraded reactor core. The final 23 hulls (SAN JUAN and later) are referred to as the Improved Los Angeles (or 688I Class). These submarines are quieter, incorporating an advanced BSY-1 sonar suite and the ability to lay mines from their torpedo tubes. Their forward diving planes were moved from the conning tower (sail) to the bow and the sail has been strengthened for breaking through ice. SALT LAKE CITY deactivated in October 2005. HONOLULU deactivated in March 2006. SAN FRANSICSO, which was heavily damaged following a collision with an undersea mountain off Guam in 2005 is to be repaired using the bow section of HONOLULU. MINNEAPOLIS-ST PAUL and HYMAN G. RICKOVER are scheduled to pay-off in 2007.

A 205-ton, large scale unmanned submarine test vehicle (CUTTHROAT LSV-2), is used to explore and test emerging technologies and to conduct physics-based experiments. Specific emphasis is on stealth, hydrodynamics, hydroacoustics and propulsion designs to permit technology insertion into current and future submarines.

LSV 2 provides the capability to develop and evaluate the effectiveness of new technologies that will result in major improvements in performance for the Virginia class submarines. LSV 2 was designed and built by an industry team from Newport News Shipbuilding and General Dynamics/Electric Boat Company under contract from Naval Sea Systems Command (NAVSEA). Delivered in 2001, LSV 2 operates on Lake Pend Oreille at the Acoustic Research Detachment in Bayview, Idaho, the Navy's laboratory for demonstrating submarine stealth technology.

US NAVYMCS2 /MIGUEL ANGEL CONTRERAS   **USS Dwight D. Eisenhower**

AIRCRAFT CARRIERS
NIMITZ CLASS

Ship	Pennant Number	Completion Date	Builder
NIMITZ	CVN 68	1975	Newport News SB
DWIGHT D. EISENHOWER	CVN 69	1977	Newport News SB
CARL VINSON	CVN 70	1982	Newport News SB
THEODORE ROOSEVELT	CVN 71	1986	Newport News SB
ABRAHAM LINCOLN	CVN 72	1989	Newport News SB
GEORGE WASHINGTON	CVN 73	1992	Newport News SB
JOHN C. STENNIS	CVN 74	1995	Newport News SB
HARRY S. TRUMAN	CVN 75	1998	Newport News SB
RONALD REAGAN	CVN 76	2003	Newport News SB
GEORGE H.W. BUSH	CVN 77	*2008*	Newport News SB

Machinery Two nuclear reactors driving four shafts **Displacement** 91,487 tons full load (CVN 68-70), 96,386 tons full load (CVN 71), 102,000 tons full load (CVN 72-74) **Dimensions** 332.9m x 40.8m x 11.3m (CVN 68-70) 11.8m (CVN 71) 11.9m (CVN 72-74) **Speed** 30+ knots **Armament** Two or three (depending on modification) NATO Sea Sparrow launchers, 20mm Phalanx CIWS mounts: (3 on CVN 68 and CVN 69, 4 on later ships.) **Aircraft** 85 **Complement** 3,200 plus 2,480 air wing.

Notes
Expected to operate for 15 years between refuellings. RONALD REAGAN has a prominent bow bulb to improve seakeeping and the island structure is one deck lower than on previous ships of the class. All have four catapults. RONALD REAGAN has larger "one piece" jet blast deflectors and flight deck operations re-orientated to the port side of the ship. A longer angled deck extension makes simultaneous landing and take off operations possible.

GEORGE H W BUSH was launched in October 2006, with delivery expected in November 2008. She is a modified-repeat of the RONALD REAGAN and will be the numerical replacement for KITTY HAWK, which retires in 2008 after 47 years of service.

Aircraft carriers subsequent to the Nimitz class will belong to the CVN 21-class, with delivery of the lead ship, GERALD FORD (CVN 78), scheduled for 2015. CVN 79, the second ship of the CVN 21, is scheduled for delivery in 2019. The CVN 21 class will incorporate such features as: a new, more efficient nuclear propulsion plant, an Electro-Magnetic Aircraft Launch System (EMALS), Advanced Arresting Gear (AAG), and a nearly three-fold increase in electrical generation capacity over that of Nimitz-class carriers. These improvements, coupled with an expanded Flight Deck and other topside changes designed to increase operational efficiency, will provide higher sortie generation rates. At the same time, manpower requirements for the ship and air wing will be significantly reduced.

Traditionally USN aircraft carriers deployed as the central unit of a Carrier Battle Group (CVBG). Today they deploy as part of a Carrier Strike Group (CSG), a smaller but more flexible force. Typically a CSG, in addition to the carrier, would comprise a cruiser, two guided-missile destroyers, an attack submarine and a supply ship. When events dictate, the CSG could be augmented by an Amphibious Group.

USS Enterprise

ENTERPRISE CLASS

Ship	Pennant Number	Completion Date	Builder
ENTERPRISE	CVN 65	1961	Newport News SB

Machinery Eight nuclear reactors driving four shafts **Displacement** 89,600 tons full load **Dimensions** 335.64m x 39.9m (75.6m flight deck width) x 11.9m **Speed** 30+ knots **Armament** Two Sea Sparrow missile launchers, three Phalanx 20 mm CIWS mounts **Aircraft** 85 **Complement** 3,350 - Air Wing 2,480.

Notes

Already over 45 years old ENTERPRISE is expected to remain in service until 2013 when she should be replaced by GERALD FORD (CVN 78). She has four rudders (as opposed to two on the Nimitz class) and eight nuclear reactors. Two are kept non-operational, reducing her top speed to 31 knots from her designed speed of 36.

USS Kitty Hawk

KITTY HAWK CLASS

Ship	Pennant Number	Completion Date	Builder
KITTY HAWK	CV 63	1961	New York SB

Machinery Eight boilers, four geared steam turbines driving four shafts, 280,000 shp **Displacement** 82,200 tons **Dimensions** 326.9m x 39.6m x 11.4m **Speed** 32 knots **Armament** Sea Sparrow launchers, 3 x 20mm Phalanx CIWS mounts **Aircraft** 85 **Complement** 3,150 plus 2,480 aircrew.

Notes

The last of the conventionally powered carriers KITTY HAWK has been based at Yokosuka, Japan, since 1998. Scheduled to retire in 2008 when she will be replaced at Yokosuka by the nuclear-powered GEORGE WASHINGTON.

USS Monterey

CRUISERS

TICONDEROGA CLASS

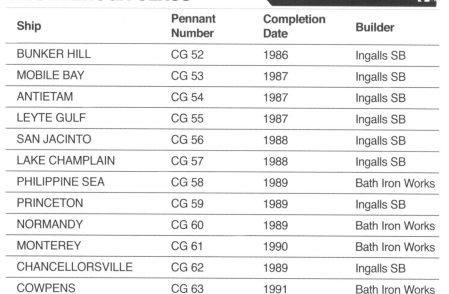

Ship	Pennant Number	Completion Date	Builder
BUNKER HILL	CG 52	1986	Ingalls SB
MOBILE BAY	CG 53	1987	Ingalls SB
ANTIETAM	CG 54	1987	Ingalls SB
LEYTE GULF	CG 55	1987	Ingalls SB
SAN JACINTO	CG 56	1988	Ingalls SB
LAKE CHAMPLAIN	CG 57	1988	Ingalls SB
PHILIPPINE SEA	CG 58	1989	Bath Iron Works
PRINCETON	CG 59	1989	Ingalls SB
NORMANDY	CG 60	1989	Bath Iron Works
MONTEREY	CG 61	1990	Bath Iron Works
CHANCELLORSVILLE	CG 62	1989	Ingalls SB
COWPENS	CG 63	1991	Bath Iron Works

Ship	Pennant Number	Completion Date	Builder
GETTYSBURG	CG 64	1991	Bath Iron Works
CHOSIN	CG 65	1991	Ingalls SB
HUE CITY	CG 66	1991	Ingalls SB
SHILOH	CG 67	1992	Bath Iron Works
ANZIO	CG 68	1992	Ingalls SB
VICKSBURG	CG 69	1992	Ingalls SB
LAKE ERIE	CG 70	1993	Bath Iron Works
CAPE ST GEORGE	CG 71	1993	Ingalls SB
VELLA GULF	CG 72	1993	Ingalls SB
PORT ROYAL	CG 73	1994	Ingalls SB

Machinery Four GE LM2500 gas turbine engines; Two shafts, 80,000 shp **Displacement** 9,600 tons **Dimensions** 172.8m x 16.8m x 9.5m **Speed** 30+ knots **Armament** Mk 41 VLS Standard Missile (MR); Vertical Launch ASROC Missile; Tomahawk Cruise Missile; Six Mk 46 torpedoes (two triple mounts); Two Mk 45 5-inch/54 calibre guns; Two Phalanx close-in-weapons systems **Aircraft** Two SH-60 Seahawk **Complement** 364

Notes

Cruisers of the USN are general purpose, or Multi-mission ships, designed to operate within a battle group. Capable of conducting anti-air, anti-submarine, anti-surface and long range strike warfare the ships usually support Carrier Strike Groups (CSG) and Expeditionary Strike Groups (ESG). They can also operate independently and as flag-ships of surface action groups. All of the early Mk 26 missile launcher fitted ships have been decommissioned, TICONDEROGA being the first to go in 2004. The remaining ships are expected to serve for at least 35 years and will be subject to the AEGIS Cruiser Modification programme which will see improvements in war-fighting capability through enhanced self defence (CIWS Block 1B, Evolved Sea Sparrow Missile (ESSM)), Cooperative Engagement Capability (CEC), improved littoral ASW capability and signif-icant land attack improvements (Tactical Tomahawk - TACTOM). A comprehensive Mission Life Extension (MLE) package will include hull, machinery and electrical system upgrades and a series of alterations designed to restore displacement and stability mar-gins, correct hull and superstructure cracking and improve accommodation spaces.

US NAVY/JO2 PATRICK REILLY

USS Arleigh Burke

DESTROYERS

ARLEIGH BURKE CLASS
Flight I & Flight II

Ship	Pennant Number	Completion Date	Builder
ARLEIGH BURKE	DDG 51	1991	Bath Iron Works
BARRY	DDG 52	1992	Ingalls SB
JOHN PAUL JONES	DDG 53	1993	Bath Iron Works
CURTIS WILBUR	DDG 54	1994	Bath Iron Works
STOUT	DDG 55	1994	Ingalls SB
JOHN S. McCAIN	DDG 56	1994	Bath Iron Works
MITSCHER	DDG 57	1995	Ingalls SB
LABOON	DDG 58	1995	Bath Iron Works
RUSSELL	DDG 59	1995	Ingalls SB
PAUL HAMILTON	DDG 60	1995	Bath Iron Works
RAMAGE	DDG 61	1995	Ingalls SB
FITZGERALD	DDG 62	1995	Bath Iron Works
STETHEM	DDG 63	1995	Ingalls SB
CARNEY	DDG 64	1996	Bath Iron Works
BENFOLD	DDG 65	1996	Ingalls SB

Ship	Pennant Number	Completion Date	Builder
GONZALEZ	DDG 66	1996	Bath Iron Works
COLE	DDG 67	1996	Ingalls SB
THE SULLIVANS	DDG 68	1997	Bath Iron Works
MILIUS	DDG 69	1996	Ingalls SB
HOPPER	DDG 70	1997	Bath Iron Works
ROSS	DDG 71	1997	Ingalls SB
MAHAN	DDG 72	1998	Bath Iron Works
DECATUR	DDG 73	1998	Bath Iron Works
McFAUL	DDG 74	1998	Ingalls SB
DONALD COOK	DDG 75	1998	Bath Iron Works
HIGGINS	DDG 76	1999	Bath Iron Works
O'KANE	DDG 77	1999	Bath Iron Works
PORTER	DDG 78	1999	Ingalls SB

Machinery Four GE LM2500-30 gas turbines; two shafts; 100,000shp **Displacement** 9,033 tons **Dimensions** 153.92m x 18m x 6.3m **Speed** 30+ knots **Armament** Mk 41 VLS Standard missile; Harpoon; VLS ASROC missiles; Tomahawk; six Mk 46 torpedoes (two triple tube mounts); one 5-inch/54 calibre gun **Aircraft** Landing facilities aft, but no hangar **Complement** 323.

Notes

Just like the cruisers, the modern day USN destroyer is a multi-mission vessel able to operate independently, or as part of a larger group, across all warfare disciplines. The combat system centres around the Aegis combat system and the SPY-1D, multi-function phased array radar. Flight II ships (from DDG 72) incorporate Link 16, SLQ 32(V) EW suite , extended range surface-air missiles and improved tactical information exchange systems. These ships also carry greater reserves of fuel, thus extending their range. The lack of an embarked helicopter on a vessel of this size has been a disadvantage and the follow-on Flight IIA ships have been redesigned to incorporate a hangar and flight deck.

The USN is introducing an Anti-Ballistic Missile programme centring around an upgraded Aegis system coupled with the SM-3 missile, providing the fleet with an ABM tracking and shoot-down capability. The requirement calls for 18 ships, of which 6 (STETHEM, DECATUR, CURTIS WILBUR and the CG-47 cruisers SHILOH, LAKE ERIE and PORT ROYAL) had received the upgrade by the end of 2006. It is expected that the ships will be employed in the Pacific.

• USS Shoup

ARLEIGH BURKE CLASS
Flight IIA

Ship	Pennant Number	Completion Date	Builder
OSCAR AUSTIN	DDG 79	2000	Bath Iron Works
ROOSEVELT	DDG 80	2000	Ingalls SB
WINSTON S. CHURCHILL	DDG 81	2001	Bath Iron Works
LASSEN	DDG 82	2001	Ingalls SB
HOWARD	DDG 83	2001	Bath Iron Works
BULKELEY	DDG 84	2001	Ingalls SB
McCAMPBELL	DDG 85	2002	Bath Iron Works
SHOUP	DDG 86	2002	Ingalls SB
MASON	DDG 87	2003	Bath Iron Works
PREBLE	DDG 88	2002	Ingalls SB

Ship	Pennant Number	Completion Date	Builder
MUSTIN	DDG 89	2003	Ingalls SB
CHAFEE	DDG 90	2003	Bath Iron Works
PINCKNEY	DDG 91	2004	Ingalls SB
MOMSEN	DDG 92	2004	Bath Iron Works
CHUNG-HOON	DDG 93	2004	Ingalls SB
NITZE	DDG 94	2004	Bath Iron Works
JAMES E. WILLIAMS	DDG 95	2004	Ingalls SB
BAINBRIDGE	DDG 96	2005	Bath Iron Works
HALSEY	DDG 97	2005	Ingalls SB
FORREST SHERMAN	DDG 98	2006	Ingalls SB
FARRAGUT	DDG 99	2006	Bath Iron Works
KIDD	DDG 100	2006	Ingalls SB
GRIDLEY	DDG 101	2006	Bath Iron Works
SAMPSON	DDG 102	2007	Bath Iron Works
TRUXTUN	DDG 103	2007	Ingalls SB
STERETT	DDG 104	2007	Bath Iron Works
DEWEY	DDG 105	2008	Ingalls SB
STOCKDALE	DDG 106	2008	Bath Iron Works
GRAVELY	DDG 107	2009	Ingalls SB

Machinery Four GE LM 2500-30 gas turbines; two shafts;100,000shp **Displacement** 9,217 tons **Dimensions** 155.3m x 20.4m x 6.3m **Speed** 30+ knots **Armament** Mk 41 VLS Standard missile; VLS ASROC missiles; Tomahawk; six Mk 46 torpedoes (two triple tube mounts); one 5-inch/54 calibre gun **Aircraft** Two SH-60 Seahawk helicopters **Complement** 323

Notes
The Flight IIA ships incorporate facilities to support two embarked helicopters, significantly enhancing the ship's sea-control capabilities . These ships have the Aegis combat system Baseline 6 Phase 3, which incorporates Cooperative Engagement Capability (CEC) and the Evolved Sea Sparrow Missile (ESSM). The Harpoon canisters have been removed as a weight saving measure, but could be re-installed, if needed, between the funnels. They have six extra VLS cells. The improved SPY- 1D(V) radar, the Remote Mine-Hunting System (RMS), as well as advanced open - architecture combat systems using commercially developed processors and display equipment were introduced as part of Baseline 7 Phase 1, commencing with DDG-91. The DDG-51 programme is planned to stop at 62 ships.

USS Nicholas

FRIGATES
OLIVER HAZARD PERRY CLASS

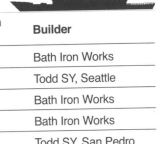

Ship	Pennant Number	Completion Date	Builder
McINERNEY	FFG 8	1979	Bath Iron Works
BOONE	FFG 28	1982	Todd SY, Seattle
STEPHEN W. GROVES	FFG 29	1982	Bath Iron Works
JOHN L. HALL	FFG 32	1982	Bath Iron Works
JARRETT	FFG 33	1983	Todd SY, San Pedro
UNDERWOOD	FFG 36	1983	Bath Iron Works
CROMMELIN	FFG 37	1983	Todd SY, Seattle
CURTS	FFG 38	1983	Todd SY, San Pedro
DOYLE	FFG 39	1983	Bath Iron Works
HALYBURTON	FFG 40	1984	Todd SY, Seattle
McCLUSKEY	FFG 41	1983	Todd SY, San Pedro
KLAKRING	FFG 42	1983	Bath Iron Works
THACH	FFG 43	1984	Todd SY, San Pedro

Ship	Pennant Number	Completion Date	Builder
DE WERT	FFG 45	1983	Bath Iron Works
RENTZ	FFG 46	1984	Todd SY, San Pedro
NICHOLAS	FFG 47	1984	Bath Iron Works
VANDEGRIFT	FFG 48	1984	Todd SY, Seattle
ROBERT G. BRADLEY	FFG 49	1984	Bath Iron Works
TAYLOR	FFG 50	1984	Bath Iron Works
GARY	FFG 51	1984	Todd SY, San Pedro
CARR	FFG 52	1985	Todd SY, Seattle
HAWES	FFG 53	1985	Bath Iron Works
FORD	FFG 54	1985	Todd SY, San Pedro
ELROD	FFG 55	1985	Bath Iron Works
SIMPSON	FFG 56	1985	Bath Iron Works
REUBEN JAMES	FFG 57	1986	Todd SY, San Pedro
SAMUEL B. ROBERTS	FFG 58	1986	Bath Iron Works
KAUFMANN	FFG 59	1987	Bath Iron Works
RODNEY M. DAVIS	FFG 60	1987	Todd SY, San Pedro
INGRAHAM	FFG 61	1989	Todd SY, San Pedro

Machinery Two GE LM2500 gas turbine engines; 1 shaft; 41,000shp **Displacement** 4,100 tonnes **Dimensions** 135.6m x 13.7m x 4.5m **Speed** 29 knots **Armament** Six Mk 46 torpedoes (two triple mounts); One 76 mm (3-inch)/62 calibre Mk 75 rapid fire gun; One Phalanx close-in-weapons system **Aircraft** Two SH-60 Seahawk **Complement** 215

Notes

Originally a class of 51 vessels, these low cost single screw frigates were designed as cost efficient surface combatants, however they lack the multi-mission capability necessary for modern surface combatants faced with multiple, high-technology threats. They also offer limited capacity for growth. They were fitted with a single Mk 13 missile launcher forward of the bridge for Harpoon and Standard missiles, but this has since been removed. Their primary role today is anti-submarine protection of amphibious groups, auxiliaries and merchant shipping. Starting with KAUFFMAN in 2003 the ships are undergoing a modernisation programme , which includes replacement of four obsolete Ship Service Diesel Generators with commercial systems and the installation of CIWS 1B and the Nulka decoy system. The programme is scheduled to complete by 2011.

USS Freedom

LITTORAL COMBAT SHIPS
FREEDOM CLASS

Ship	Pennant Number	Completion Date	Builder
FREEDOM	LCS 1	2007	LM/Marinette Marine Shipyard
NOT YET NAMED	LCS 3	2009	Bollinger, LA

Machinery Combined diesel and gas turbine with steerable water jet propulsion **Displacement** 3,000 tonnes **Dimensions** 115m x 13m x 4m **Speed** 45+ knots **Armament** One Bofors 57mm; one RAM launcher; four .50 calibre MG; additional weapons can be added depending on role **Complement** 15 core crew (up to 75 max.)

Notes
One of two designs being constructed under a 2006 contract . The contract for the Flight 0 vessels is for two vessels of each design, with an ultimate requirement for up to 60 vessels. The Lockheed Martin design is for a semi-planing steel mono-hull. The vessels weapons and sensor packages will be of a modular design, allowing the vessels to be re-roled within a very short space of time (as quickly as 24 hours in some cases). They can be equipped for anti-surface, anti-submarine, mine warfare or surveillance duties. FREEDOM will be manned by one of two rotational crews, blue and gold, similar to the rotational crews assigned to Trident submarines. The crews will be augmented by one of three mission package crews during focused mission assignments FREEDOM was christened on 23 September 2006. Orders for Flight 1 (second generation) vessels are expected to be placed in 2008/09 with delivery scheduled for 2010/12. All vessels are to bear the names of small and medium sized US cities. The first four vessels are to be based at San Diego.

INDEPENDENCE CLASS

Ship	Pennant Number	Completion Date	Builder
INDEPENDENCE	LCS 2	2008	GD/ Austal USA
NOT YET NAMED	LCS 4		GD/ Austal USA

Machinery Combined diesel and Gas Turbines with steerable waterjet propulsion **Displacement** 2,880 tonnes **Dimensions** 127.1m x 30.4m x 4.5m **Speed** 45 knots **Armament** One Bofors 57mm; one RAM launcher; four .50 calibre MG; additional weapons can be added depending on role **Complement** 50 core crew (up to 75)

Notes
An aluminium trimaran design from Austal/General Dynamics, offering a large flight deck and helicopter handling capability on a relatively small displacement vessel, the hangar being able to accommodate two Seahawk helicopters, while the flight deck can handle helicopters the size of the CH-53 Sea Stallion.

A Mine Warfare mission package should be delivered in 2007 with Anti-submarine Warfare and Surface Warfare packages being delivered in 2008.

USS Guardian

MINE COUNTERMEASURES SHIPS
AVENGER CLASS

Ship	Pennant Number	Completion Date	Builder
AVENGER	MCM 1	1987	Peterson Builders Inc.
DEFENDER	MCM 2	1989	Marinette Marine Corp.
SENTRY	MCM 3	1989	Peterson Builders Inc.
CHAMPION	MCM 4	1991	Marinette Marine Corp.
GUARDIAN	MCM 5	1989	Peterson Builders Inc.
DEVASTATOR	MCM 6	1990	Peterson Builders Inc.
PATRIOT	MCM 7	1991	Marinette Marine Corp.
SCOUT	MCM 8	1990	Peterson Builders Inc.
PIONEER	MCM 9	1992	Peterson Builders Inc.
WARRIOR	MCM 10	1993	Peterson Builders Inc.
GLADIATOR	MCM 11	1993	Peterson Builders Inc.
ARDENT	MCM 12	1994	Peterson Builders Inc.
DEXTROUS	MCM 13	1994	Peterson Builders Inc.
CHIEF	MCM 14	1994	Peterson Builders Inc.

Machinery Four diesels (each 600shp); two shafts with controllable pitch propellers **Displacement** 1,450 tons **Dimensions** 68.4m x 11.9m x 3.7m **Speed** 13.5 knots **Armament** 2 x 12.7 MG (MCM11 1 x 25mm 88 Bushmaster; 1 x 7.63 Gatling MG) **Complement** 84.

Notes

Designed as minehunter-killers capable of finding, classifying and destroying moored and bottom mines. They retain a conventional minesweeping capability. Can deploy and operate independently. The hull of the ships are constructed of oak, Douglas Fir and Alaskan Cedar, with a thin coating of fibreglass to take advantage of wood's low magnetic signature during mine countermeasures operations.

The class has been undergoing a modernization programme since 2004 aimed at correcting maintenance and obsolescence issues. The MCM-1 modernization package includes Planned Product Improvement Programme (PPIP) on the Isotta Fraschini main engines and generators for MCM-3 through MCM-14; replacement of the obsolete Mine Neutralization Vehicle with a commercial Expendable Mine Neutralization System (EMNS); and upgrading the existing SQQ-32 Sonar with High Frequency Wide Band capabilities. Other major HM&E alterations include 400-Hz modifications, replacement of Aft Deck hydraulic equipment with electric equipment, replacement of the diesel generator analogue voltage regulators with digital voltage regulators, and upgrading the common navigation system. The modernization effort is scheduled for completion by 2010.

Of the 14 ships built, nine remain in active service, and five are in the Naval Reserve Fleet (AVENGER, DEFENDER, SENTRY, CHAMPION and GLADIATOR). Upon decommissioning of the ten MHC-51 Osprey-class Coastal Mine Hunters, the five Naval Reserve Fleet ships will be placed back into active service. PATRIOT and GUARDIAN are forward deployed to Sasebo, Japan.

USS Raven

COASTAL MINE HUNTERS
OSPREY CLASS

Ship	Pennant Number	Completion Date	Builder
HERON	MHC 52	1994	Intermarine, Savannah
PELICAN	MHC 53	1995	Avondale Industries
KINGFISHER	MHC 56	1996	Avondale Industries
CORMORANT	MHC 57	1997	Avondale Industries
BLACK HAWK	MHC 58	1996	Intermarine, Savannah
CARDINAL	MHC 60	1997	Intermarine, Savannah
RAVEN	MHC 61	1998	Intermarine, Savannah
SHRIKE	MHC 62	1999	Intermarine, Savannah

Machinery Two diesels (each 800 shp); two Voith Schneider (cycloidal) propulsion systems **Displacement** 890 tons **Dimensions** 57.3m x 10.9m x 3.4m **Speed** 12 knots **Armament** 1 - 30mm gun **Complement** 51

Notes

The Osprey class are the world's largest glass-reinforced plastic (GRP) ships and have a similar role to the larger Avenger class, though having a limited endurance (15 days) making them reliant on a support vessel or shore facilities during operations. The design is based on the Italian Navy Lerici Class with Voith-Schneider vertical propulsors as oppossed to the traditional propeller and rudder arrangements of earlier ships. All except CARDINAL and RAVEN are operated by the US Navy Reserves.

All 12 Osprey class will be phased out by 2008, being replaced by the Littoral Combat Ships which will carry minehunting equipment. A Bill put before congress in 2005 sought the transfer by grant, of PELICAN to Greece and CARDINAL and RAVEN to Egypt. The same bill sought to transfer by sale HERON to Greece. A further Bill for 2007 sought approval for the transefer of KINGFISHER and CORMORANT to Lithuania (by grant), ORIOLE and FALCON to Taiwan (by sale) and SHRIKE and BLACK HAWK (one by grant and one by sale) to Turkey.

OSPREY, ROBIN, ORIOLE and FALCON were decommissioned in 2006.

US NAVY/PH1 ROBERT McRILL **USS Sirocco**

PATROL SHIPS (COASTAL)
CYCLONE CLASS

Ship	Pennant Number	Completion Date	Builder
HURRICANE	PC 3	1993	Bollinger, Lockport
TYPHOON	PC 5	1994	Bollinger, Lockport
SIROCCO	PC 6	1994	Bollinger, Lockport
SQUALL	PC 7	1994	Bollinger, Lockport
CHINOOK	PC 9	1995	Bollinger, Lockport
FIREBOLT	PC 10	1995	Bollinger, Lockport
WHIRLWIND	PC 11	1995	Bollinger, Lockport
THUNDERBOLT	PC 12	1995	Bollinger, Lockport

Machinery Four Paxman diesels; four shafts; 3,350 shp **Displacement** 336 tonnes **Dimensions** 51.8m x 7.6m x 2.4m **Speed** 35 knots **Armament** One Mk 96 and one Mk 38 25mm MG; Five .50 calibre MG; two Mk 19 40mm automatic grenade launchers; Two M-60 machine guns **Complement** 28

Notes

At one time this was a class of ship looking for a role within the "blue water" US Navy. Now, with a shift of emphasis to littoral operations, these coastal patrol craft have become key players in the patrol, interdiction and surveillance roles in a shallow water environment. Six vessels are stationed at NAB Little Creek on the Atlantic coast and two at NAB Coronado, on the Pacific coast. TYPHOON and SCIROCCO are deployed to the Gulf and crews are rotated from both bases. On 30 September 2004 TEMPEST (PC 2), MONSOON, (PC 4), ZEPHYR, (PC 8), SHAMAL, (PC 13) and TORNADA, (PC 14) were decommissioned and transferred to the U.S. Coast Guard, on loan for four years. The Navy retain ownership of the vessels and are responsible for maintenance. CYCLONE (PC 1) was transferred to the Philippine Navy in 2003.

Sea Ark

INSHORE BOAT UNITS

Naval Coastal Warfare Squadrons (NCWRON) are undergoing a rapid expansion as Homeland and Port security have taken on a greater importance since the terror attacks of 9/11. Traditionally a reservist function, the NCWRONs have been so successful that the USN is forming eight active duty squadrons. The new units comprise 580 personnel organised into squadrons operating from San Diego and Norfolk. Reserve NCWRONs total 3,500 personnel in 45 units

Each NCWRON, is comprised of a Mobile Inshore Undersea Warfare Unit, Inshore Boat Units (IBU) and staff. Each IBU is equipped with six small, fast and heavily armed boats, that are able to be deployed rapidly by air. The overall mission of the IBUs is to conduct port security, coastal surveillance and interception as necessary, as well as to protect maritime assets and infrastructure. This includes ships, submarines, piers, ports, oil platforms or a new beachead for delivering supplies to support humanitarian assistance. IBUs also co-ordinate their efforts with USCG Port Security Units.

Inshore Boat Units are deployed on anti-terrorism and force protection duties in harbours and coastal waterways in the continental United States and at overseas locations such as Korea, the Gulf and the Horn of Africa region.

USS Essex

AMPHIBIOUS ASSAULT SHIPS (LHD/LHA)

WASP CLASS

Ship	Pennant Number	Comm Date	Builder
WASP	LHD 1	1989	Ingalls SB
ESSEX	LHD 2	1992	Ingalls SB
KEARSARGE	LHD 3	1993	Ingalls SB
BOXER	LHD 4	1995	Ingalls SB
BATAAN	LHD 5	1997	Ingalls SB
BONHOMME RICHARD	LHD 6	1998	Ingalls SB
IWO JIMA	LHD 7	2001	Ingalls SB
MAKIN ISLAND	LHD 8	2007	Ingalls SB

Machinery Two boilers; two geared steam turbines driving two shafts; 70,000shp **Displacement** 40,650 tons (LHD 1-4); 40,358 (LHD 5-7); 41,772 (LHD 8) **Dimensions** 257.3m x 32.3m x 8.1m **Speed** 22 knots **Armament** Two RAM launchers; two NATO Sea Sparrow launchers; three 20mm Phalanx CIWS mounts (two on LHD 5-7); four .50 cal. MG; four 25 mm Mk 38 MG (LHD 5-7 have three 25 mm Mk 38 MG) **Aircraft** 12 CH-46 Sea Knight helicopters; 4 CH-53E Sea Stallion helicopters; 6 AV-8B Harrier attack aircraft; 3 UH-1N Huey helicopters; 4 AH-1W Super Cobra helicopters **Complement** 1108 (+1894 Marines)

Notes

The largest of all amphibious warfare ships the LHD resembles a small aircraft carrier; capable of operating V/STOL aircraft, CV-22 Osprey tiltrotor and conventional helicopters. The ships also have a well deck in which three Landing Craft Air Cushion (LCAC) and other watercraft can be carried. These ships were the last major ships in the USN to be built with steam turbines. MAKIN ISLAND is to be completed with a gas turbine powerplant. They have extensive medical facilities comprising six fully equipped operating theatres and a 600 bed hospital.

The aircraft mix depends upon the ships mission, but it can include up to 42 CH-46 Sea Knight helicopters in the pure assault role or 20 AV-8B Harriers and 6 ASW helicopters in the Sea Control mission.

Traditionally USN amphibious ships deployed as part of an Amphibious Ready Group (ARG), which typically comprised a LHD or LHA, supported by LPDs and LSDs. The ARG would then come under the umbrella of a Carrier Battle Group. Deployment patterns are now changing and the Amphibious ships now deploy as an Expeditionary Strike Group (ESG). This is still centred around the usual elements of an ARG, but now include, their own escort and strike package comprising a guided missile cruiser armed with Tomahawk missiles, a guided missile destroyer, a frigate and a nuclear-powered submarine.

USS Peleliu

TARAWA CLASS

Ship	Pennant Number	Completion Date	Builder
TARAWA	LHA 1	1976	Ingalls SB
SAIPAN	LHA 2	1977	Ingalls SB
NASSAU	LHA 4	1978	Ingalls SB
PELELIU	LHA 5	1978	Ingalls SB

Machinery Two boilers; two geared steam turbines driving two shafts; 70,000shp **Displacement** 39,400 tons **Dimensions** 249.9m x 31.8m x 7.9m **Speed** 24 knots **Armament** Two RAM launchers; two Phalanx 20 mm CIWS mount; three .50 cal. MG; four 25 mm Mk 38 MG **Aircraft** 2 CH-46 Sea Knight helicopters; 4 CH-53E Sea Stallion helicopters; 6 AV-8B Harrier attack aircraft; 3 UH-1N Huey helicopters; 4 AH-1W Super Cobra helicopters **Complement** 964 (Marine Detachment 1,900 plus).

Notes
From an original class of five (BELLEAU WOOD decommissioned on 28 Oct 2005 and was sunk as a target during Exercise RIMPAC 2006) these ships are to be replaced under the LHA(R) programme which is scheduled to deliver the first ship in 2013. To be around 50,000 tonnes and gas turbine powered they will be designed to operate the MV-22 Osprey and the new F-35B Joint Strike Fighter. SAIPAN is scheduled to decommission in April 2007 after which she will be used for a series of "experiments".

USS Blue Ridge

AMPHIBIOUS COMMAND SHIPS
BLUE RIDGE CLASS

Ship	Pennant Number	Completion Date	Builder
BLUE RIDGE	LCC 19	1970	Philadelphia Naval SY
MOUNT WHITNEY	LCC 20	1971	Newport News SB

Machinery Two boilers; one geared steam turbines driving one shaft; 22,000shp **Displacement** 18,874 tons **Dimensions** 190m x 32m x 8.8m **Speed** 23 knots **Armament** 2 x Phalanx CIWS **Complement** 842

Notes

As opposed to earlier Amphibious Command Ships which were conversions of earlier vessels, these two ships were designed specifically for the role. Earlier amphibious command ships lacked sufficient speed to keep up with a 20-knot amphibious force. Both ships now serve as fleet flagships. USS BLUE RIDGE became the Seventh Fleet command ship in 1979, and USS MOUNT WHITNEY became the Second Fleet command ship in 1981, and the Sixth Fleet command ship in February 2005. Although commanded by a USN officer and having a USN mission crew, navigation, seamanship, engineering, laundry and galley services are provided by Military Sealift Command civil service mariners.

USS San Antonio

AMPHIBIOUS TRANSPORT DOCK (LPD)

SAN ANTONIO CLASS

Ship	Pennant Number	Comm Date	Builder
SAN ANTONIO	LPD 17	2006	Northrop Grumman SS Avondale
NEW ORLEANS	LPD 18	2006	Northrop Grumman SS Avondale
MESA VERDE	LPD 19	2006	Northrop Grumman SS Pascagoula
GREEN BAY	LPD 20	2006	Northrop Grumman SS Avondale
NEW YORK	LPD 21	2007	Northrop Grumman SS Avondale
SAN DIEGO	LPD 22	*2010*	Northrop Grumman SS Avondale
ANCHORAGE	LPD 23	*2011*	Northrop Grumman SS Avondale
ARLINGTON	LPD 24	*2011*	Northrop Grumman SS Pascagoula
SOMERSET	LPD 25		

Machinery Four sequentially turbo-charged marine Colt-Pielstick diesels driving two shafts; 41,600shp **Displacement** 25,300 tonnes **Dimensions** 208.5m x 31.9m x 7m **Speed** 22+ knots **Armament** Two Bushmaster II 30 mm Close in Guns; two Rolling

46

Airframe Missile launchers **Aircraft** Launch or land two CH53E Super Stallion helicopters or two MV-22 Osprey tilt-rotor aircraft or up to four CH-46 Sea Knight helicopters, AH-1 or UH-1 helicopters **Complement** 360 (Embarked landing force 720 - surge capacity to 800)

Notes

The 12-ship LPD 17 programme serves as the functional replacement for the Austin class LPD, Anchorage class LSD, Newport class LST and Charleston class LKA. The initial contract award to design and build the lead ship of the class was awarded to the Avondale-Bath Alliance in December 1996. A contract award protest was successfully resolved in April 1997. LPD 17 class workload was transferred from Bath Iron Works to Northrop Grumman Ship Systems (NGSS) in June 2002.

The ships have 25,000 square feet of space for vehicles (more than twice that of the Austin class), 34,000 cubic feet for cargo, accommodation for approximately 720 troops (800 surge), and a medical facility (24 beds and four operating rooms-two medical and two dental). The aft well deck can launch and recover traditional surface assault craft as well as two landing craft air cushion (LCAC) vehicles, capable of transporting cargo, personnel, Marine vehicles, and tanks, and the Marine Corps' new Expeditionary Fighting Vehicle (EFV). Aviation facilities include a hangar and flight deck (33 percent larger than Austin class) in order to operate and maintain a variety of aircraft, including current and future rotary-wing aircraft. Other advanced features include the Advance Enclosed Mast/Sensor (AEM/S) for reduced signature/sensor maintenance, reduced-signature composite-material enclosed masts, other stealth enhancements, state-of-the-art C4ISR and self-defence systems, a Shipboard Wide-Area Network (SWAN) that will link shipboard systems and embarked Marine Corps units, and significant quality of life improvements for the ships company.

The programme has been plagued by reports of poor workmanship, late delivery and rising budgets. At present (2007) LPDs 17 through 21 are under construction: SAN ANTONIO was delivered in July 2005 and commissioned in January 2006. NEW ORLEANS, started construction in February 2002, and was expected to deliver in December 2005. MESA VERDE started construction at NGSS Pascagoula in August 2002, and was to deliver in 2006. GREEN BAY started construction in March 2003 and is expected to deliver in 2007. NEW YORK started construction in March 2004 and is expected to deliver in 2008. Contract negotiations for SAN DIEGO, ANCHORAGE, and ARLINGTON are ongoing. LPD 24 and LPD 25 are named ARLINGTON and SOMERSET respectively to honour the heroes and victims of the 11 September 2001 Pentagon attack and the flight downed in Pennsylvania.

USS Cleveland

AUSTIN CLASS

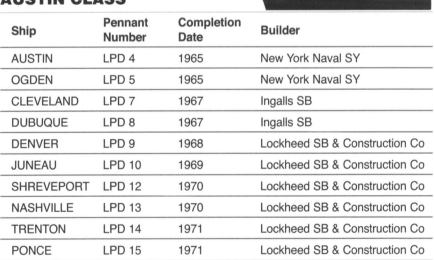

Ship	Pennant Number	Completion Date	Builder
AUSTIN	LPD 4	1965	New York Naval SY
OGDEN	LPD 5	1965	New York Naval SY
CLEVELAND	LPD 7	1967	Ingalls SB
DUBUQUE	LPD 8	1967	Ingalls SB
DENVER	LPD 9	1968	Lockheed SB & Construction Co
JUNEAU	LPD 10	1969	Lockheed SB & Construction Co
SHREVEPORT	LPD 12	1970	Lockheed SB & Construction Co
NASHVILLE	LPD 13	1970	Lockheed SB & Construction Co
TRENTON	LPD 14	1971	Lockheed SB & Construction Co
PONCE	LPD 15	1971	Lockheed SB & Construction Co

Machinery Two boilers, two steam turbines driving two shafts; 24,000shp **Displacement** 17,272 tonnes **Dimensions** 171m x 25.2m x 7m **Speed** 21 knots **Armament** Two 25mm Mk 38 guns; two Phalanx CIWS; and eight .50-calibre MG **Aircraft** Up to six CH-46 Sea Knight helicopters **Complement** 420 (Marine Detachment 900)

Notes

The versatile Austin-class LPDs, a lengthened version of the earlier Raleigh class, provide substantial amphibious lift for USMC troops and their vehicles and cargo. Additionally, they serve as the secondary aviation platform for Expeditionary Strike Groups, having a large flight deck capable of operating up to six CH-46 Sea Knight, or three CH-53 Sea Stallion helicopters . A small telescoping hangar, suitable only for a small utility helicopter, is fitted to all except AUSTIN. A well deck can accommodate one landing craft air cushion (LCAC), or one utility landing craft (LCU), or four mechanized landing craft (LCU). Ships can accommodate up to 900 troops and carry 2,000 tons of supplies and equipment. LPD-7 to LPD-13 have an extra superstructure level enabling them to operate as flagships. All are to be replaced by the San Antonio class LPD. AUSTIN decommissioned in September 2006 and SHREVEPORT was to decommission by the end of the year. In 2007 TRENTON is to be transferred to the Indian Navy, together with four LCMs for a reported cost of $48 million. Approval has been sought to transfer OGDEN and CLEVELAND to Mexico when they decommission in 2007.

USS Coronado

COMMAND SHIP
CORONADO CLASS

Ship	Pennant Number	Completion Date	Builder
CORONADO	AGF 11	1970	Lockheed

Machinery Two boilers, two geared steam turbines driving two shafts: 24,000shp **Displacement** 17,183 tonnes **Dimensions** 173.8m x 30.5m x 7m **Speed** 21 knots **Armament** Two Phalanx CIWS, two 12.7 mm MG **Aircraft** Two light helicopters **Complement** 516 (plus 120 flag staff).

Notes

The ship was decommissioned and transfered to Military Sealift Command in February 2005. Navigation, seamanship, engineering, laundry and galley services are provided by MSC civil service mariners. The ship is at reduced operating status (30 days notice) A USN commanding officer and USN mission crew are embarked when the ship is fully operational. The ship was scheduled to decommission in September 2006.

US NAVY/PAUL FARLEY   **USS Ashland**

WHIDBEY ISLAND CLASS

Ship	Pennant Number	Completion Date	Builder
WHIDBEY ISLAND	LSD 41	1985	Lockheed SB & Construction Co
GERMANTOWN	LSD 42	1986	Lockheed SB & Construction Co
FORT McHENRY	LSD 43	1987	Lockheed SB & Construction Co
GUNSTON HALL	LSD 44	1989	Avondale Industries
COMSTOCK	LSD 45	1990	Avondale Industries
TORTUGA	LSD 46	1990	Avondale Industries
RUSHMORE	LSD 47	1991	Avondale Industries
ASHLAND	LSD 48	1992	Avondale Industries

Machinery Four Colt Industries, 16 Cylinder diesels driving two shafts; 33,000shp **Displacement** 15, 726 tonnes **Dimensions** 185.6m x 25.6m x 6.3m **Speed** 20+ knots **Armament** Two 25mm Mk 38 MG; Two 20mm Phalanx CIWS mounts and Six .50 cal. MG **Landing Craft** Four Landing Craft Air Cushion (LCAC) **Complement** 413 (Marine Detachment 402 plus 102 surge)

Notes

The LSD 41 class was designed specifically to operate Landing Craft Air Cushion (LCAC) vessels - basically gas turbine powered cargo-carrying hovercraft, and it has the largest capacity for these landing craft (four) of any USN amphibious ship. The ships can ballast down in 15 minutes and deballast in 30, providing a depth of water of 6ft forward and 10 foot aft for operating landing craft. The flight deck is raised above the 440 ft long docking well in order to provide all-around ventilation for the gas turbine-engined LCACs. There are two landing spots on the flight deck for up to CH-53-sized helicopters but no hangar facilities. The ships carry 90 tons JP-5 fuel for helicopters. Medical facilities include an operating room and 8 beds. In an effort to enhance the ship's ability to counter the cruise missile threat Phalanx CIWS and RAM missile systems are being progressively fitted throughout the class.

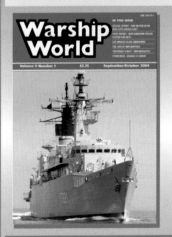

USS Pearl Harbor

DOCK LANDING SHIP (LSD)
HARPERS FERRY CLASS

Ship	Pennant Number	Commission Date	Builder
HARPERS FERRY	LSD 49	1995	Avondale Industries
CARTER HALL	LSD 50	1995	Avondale Industries
OAK HILL	LSD 51	1996	Avondale Industries
PEARL HARBOR	LSD 52	1998	Avondale Industries

Machinery Four Colt Industries, 16 Cylinder diesels driving two shafts; 33,000shp **Displacement** 16,976 tonnes **Dimensions** 185.6m x 25.6m x 6.3m **Speed** 20+ knots **Armament** Two 25mm Mk 38 MF, Two 20mm Phalanx CIWS mounts and Six .50 cal. MG **Landing Craft** Two Landing Craft Air Cushion (LCAC) **Complement** 419 (Marine Detachment 402 plus 102 surge)

Notes

Similar in all respects to the Whidbey Island class, these four vessels were optimised for the cargo carrying role. The ships differ from the original LSD 41 by reducing the number of LCACs to two in favour of additional cargo capacity. The well deck has been shortened and the portside crane removed.

LCAC-41

LANDING CRAFT AIR CUSHION (LCAC)

Machinery 4x Allied-Signal TF-40B gas turbines (2 for propulsion/2 for lift); 16,000 hp sustained; 2 x shrouded reversible pitch airscrews; 4 x double-entry fans, centrifugal or mixed flow (lift); 4 x Vericor Power Systems ETF-40B gas turbines with Full Authority Digital Engine Control (FADEC) **Displacement** 185 tonnes **Dimensions** 26.4m x 14.3m **Speed** 40+ knots **Armament** 12.7mm MGs. Gun mounts will support: M2HB .50 cal machine gun; Mk 19 Mod3 40mm grenade launcher; M60 MG **Range** 200 miles at 40 kts with payload / 300 miles at 35 kts with payload **Load** 60 tons / 75 ton overload **Military Lift** 24 troops or 1 Main Battle Tank **Complement** 5

Notes

91 LCACs were built between 1984 and 2001, production being split between Textron Marine and Land Systems and Avondale Gulfport Marine. The LCAC is a high-speed, over-the-beach fully amphibious landing craft, capable of carrying a 60-75 ton payload. It is used to transport the weapons systems, equipment, cargo and personnel of the assault elements of the Marine Air-Ground Task Force from ship to shore and across the beach. Its air cushion design allows it to access more than 70% of the world's coastline. LCACs are transported in, and can be deployed from, any USN amphibious ship equipped with a well deck. In recent years these craft have proved themselves invaluable in providing humanitarian relief to areas devastated by tsunami and hurricane, being able to access remote areas. A Service Life Extension Programme (SLEP) to extend hull life from 20 to 30 years for 73 of the 82 active LCACs will be accomplished through 2017. Nine craft that were in reduced operating status were deleted in 2006. A replacement programme, imaginatively titled the Seabase to Shore Connector (SSC), is expected to deliver a vessel capable of lifting 144 tons by 2015.

• US NAVY/PH2 BRANDON A. TEEPLES

LCU-1630

LANDING CRAFT
UTILITY (LCU) 1600 CLASS

Machinery 2 x Detroit 12V-71 Diesel engines, twin shaft, 680 hp sustained, Kort nozzles **Displacement** 381 tonnes **Dimensions** 41.1m x 8.8m x 2m **Speed** 12 knots **Armament** 12.7mm MGs **Range** 190 miles at 9 kts with full load **Load** 180 tons **Military Lift** 125 tons of cargo **Complement** 14

Notes

Powered by two diesel engines driving twin shafts, LCUs are able to transport tracked or wheeled vehicles and troops from amphibious assault ships to beachheads or piers and have both bow and stern ramps for onload/offload at either end. The LCU 1600 class were built from the 1960's through to the 1980's and are still used to transport those loads too heavy for the LCACs, being able to transport up to three M-60 tanks or 400 troops. LCUs are also able to operate independently of their mother ships and are equipped with accommodation spaces for the crew. Similar craft are operated by the US Army.

HSV Swift

HIGH SPEED VESSEL

Ship	Pennant Number	Commission Date	Builder
SWIFT	HSV 2	2003	Bollinger/IncatUSA

Machinery Caterpillar 3618 marine Diesel engines **Displacement** 700 Dwt **Dimensions** 98m x 27m x 3.4m **Speed** 45+ knots **Armament** 25mm Mk 96 gun **Range** 4000+ miles **Load** 605 tons **Complement** 42

Notes
A high-speed catamaran, SWIFT was delivered to the USN only 10 months after the contract for her construction was awarded. Drawing on experience gained from JOINT VENTURE (HSV-X1) and the Army's high-speed theatre support vessel SPEARHEAD (TSV-1X) will be used to develop concepts in support of the Littoral Combat Ship (LCS) programme. SWIFT is currently serving operationally as an interim Mine Warfare Command and Support Ship (MCS) and Navy/Marine Corps experimentation vessel.

JOINT VENTURE is employed by Special Operations Command as a proof-of-concept platform for an afloat special operations platform in the western Pacific. JOINT VENTURE has the capability to facilitate company-sized units and its modifications include a helicopter landing deck along with a military command, control and communications suite.

USS Emory S. Land

SUBMARINE TENDERS
L.Y. SPEAR CLASS

Ship	Pennant Number	Completion Date	Builder
EMORY S. LAND	AS 39	1979	Lockheed SB & Construction Co
FRANK CABLE	AS 40	1980	Lockheed SB & Construction Co

Machinery Two boilers; two geared steam turbines driving one shaft; 20,000shp
Displacement 23,493 tonnes **Dimensions** 196.2m x 25.9m x 8.7m **Speed** 20 knots
Armament Four 20mm Mk 67 Oerlikon **Complement** 587 (plus 94 Flag Staff)

Notes

The L.Y. Spear class is designed and equipped to support nuclear-powered attack submarines and can service up to four submarines berthed alongside simultaneously. The ship's capabilities include: nuclear system repair and testing, electrical and electronic repair, hull repair, sheet metal and steel work, pipe fabrication, foundry, woodworking, underwater diving and rescue, and hazardous material management. Various services are available to all submarines alongside including steam, diesel fuel, water, and electricity. The ships are capable of handling and storing submarine launched weapons. In addition they provide living quarters for more than 1500 people and are equipped with full medical and dental facilities, laundry and dry cleaning plants, data processing equipment and large storage areas for refrigerated and dry cargo food. They have one 30 ton crane and two mobile cranes. AS 40 is forward deployed at Guam. With the closure of the base at La Maddalena, Italy, AS 39 will return to Bremerton for overhaul in 2007. On completion of the overhaul in 2008 she will be transferred to the Military Sealift Command.

USS Safeguard

RESCUE AND SALVAGE VESSELS
SAFEGUARD CLASS

Ship	Pennant Number	Completion Date	Builder
SAFEGUARD	ARS 50	1985	Peterson Builders Inc

Machinery Four Caterpillar 399 diesels driving two shafts 4,200shp **Displacement** 2,880 tonnes **Dimensions** 77.7m x 15.5m x 5.2m **Speed** 14 knots **Armament** Two Mk 38 25mm guns **Complement** 96

Notes

The USN has responsibility for salvaging US government-owned ships and, when it is in the best interests of the United States, privately-owned vessels as well. For rescue missions, these ships are equipped with fire monitors forward and amidships which can deliver either firefighting foam or sea water. The salvage holds are outfitted with portable equipment to provide assistance to other vessels in pumping out, patching, supply of electrical power and other essential services required to return a disabled ship to an operating condition. Equipped with a recompression chamber. SAFEGUARD is forward deployed to Sasebo, Japan. GRASP, GRAPPLE and SALVOR have been transferred to the Military Sealift Command. SAFEGUARD is scheduled to transfer to the MSC in September 2007.

USS NR-1

MISCELLANEOUS VESSELS
RESEARCH SUBMARINE

Ship	Pennant Number	Completion Date	Builder
NR-1	NR 1	1969	GD Electric Boat Division

Machinery One nuclear reactor **Displacement** 400 tons **Dimensions** 45.72m x 4.18m x 4.5m **Speed** 4 knots **Complement** 13

Notes
The first deep submergence vessel using nuclear power, it maneouvers by four ducted thrusters, two in the bow and two in the stern. The vessel also has planes mounted on the sail, and a conventional rudder. Its features include extendable bottoming wheels, three viewing ports, exterior lighting and television and still cameras for colour photographic studies, an object recovery claw, a manipulator that can be fitted with various gripping and cutting tools and a work basket that can be used in conjunction with the manipulator to deposit or recover items in the sea. The submarine requires a surface "mother ship" to support her.

USS Dolphin

RESEARCH SUBMARINE

Ship	Pennant Number	Completion Date	Builder
DOLPHIN	AGSS 555	1968	Portsmouth Naval SY

Machinery Diesel/Electric; Two GM 12-cylinder, 425 hp engines. **Displacement** 950 tons **Dimensions** 46.3m x 5.9m x 5.5m **Speed** 15+ knots (dived) **Complement** 37

Notes
The only operational, diesel-electric, deep-diving, research and development submarine in the USN. Because she was designed as a test platform, the submarine can be modified both internally and externally to allow installation of up to 12 tons of special research and test equipment. The submarine has internal and external mounting points, multiple electronic hull connectors, and up to 10 equipment racks for project use. In 2002 the vessel suffered fire and flooding damage 100 miles off the coast of San Diego. Although evacuated by the crew she was eventually escorted back to port where she underwent an extensive $60 million refit, returning to service in 2005. Following a surprise announcement she was paid off in December 2006 and is to be sunk during a fleet training exercise.

USS Mystic

DEEP SUBMERGENCE RESCUE VESSEL
MYSTIC CLASS

Ship	Pennant Number	Completion Date	Builder
MYSTIC	DSRV 1	1971	Lockheed Missile & Space Co.
AVALON	DSRV 2	1972	Lockheed Missile & Space Co.

Machinery Electric motors driving one shaft; four thrusters **Displacement** 38 tons **Dimensions** 15m x 2.4m **Speed** 4 knots **Depth** 5,000 ft **Complement** 2 pilots, 2 rescue personnel and capacity for 24 passengers

Notes
DSRVs were developed as a result of the USS THRESHER submarine accident in 1963, when all hands were lost. At the time, submarine operating depths greatly exceeded the capabilities of rescue vessels. The two DSRVs are designed to perform rescue operations on submerged, disabled submarines of the USN or foreign navies. They are designed for quick deployment in the event of a submarine accident, being transportable by lorry, aircraft, ship, or by specially configured attack submarine. At the accident site, the DSRV works with either a "mother" ship or "mother" submarine. The DSRV dives, conducts a sonar search, and attaches itself to the disabled submarine's hatch. DSRVs can embark up to 24 personnel for transfer to the "mother" vessel. They are equipped with an arm to clear hatches on a disabled submarine and a combined gripper and cable cutter. The gripper is able to lift 1,000 pounds.

Sea Fighter

EXPERIMENTAL CRAFT
SEA FIGHTER

Ship	Pennant Number	Completion Date	Builder
SEA FIGHTER	FSF-1	2005	Nichols Brothers Boat Builders

Machinery Two GE LM2500 Gas Turbines; two MTU diesels driving four Rolls-Royce waterjets **Displacement** 950 tons **Dimensions** 79.9m x 22m x 3.5m **Speed** 50+ knots **Complement** 26

Notes

The Littoral Surface Craft-Experimental LSC(X) was developed by the Office of Naval Research and christened SEA FIGHTER (FSF 1) on 5 February 2005. This high speed aluminum catamaran will test a variety of technologies that will allow the USN to operate in littoral waters. Following approximately two months of trials, SEA FIGHTER was delivered at the end of April 2005. Operational control rests with the USN's Third Fleet with the ship operating out of San Diego, CA. SEA FIGHTER is used to evaluate the hydrodynamic performance, structural behaviour, mission flexibility, and propulsion system efficiency of high speed vessels.

USS Sea Shadow

EXPERIMENTAL VESSEL
SEA SHADOW

Ship	Pennant Number	Completion Date	Builder
SEA SHADOW	IX-529	1983	Lockheed SB Corporation

Machinery Diesel Electric **Displacement** 560 tons **Dimensions** 50m x 21m x 4.4m
Speed 9 knots **Complement** 12 (plus 12 technicians)

Notes
SEA SHADOW is a test craft developed under a combined programme by the Advanced Research Projects Agency (ARPA), the Navy, and Lockheed Martin Missiles and Space Company. Of SWATH design, with the sides angled at 45° to reduce radar cross section. Begun in the mid-1980s, its purpose is to explore a variety of new technologies for surface ships, including ship control, structures, automation for reduced manning, seakeeping and signature reduction. The vessel was built in secret, inside HMB-1, a covered, semi-submersible mining barge, which subsequently became its base for operations. The vessel was laid up in 1986 and reactivated between 1993-95. Reactivated again in 1999, the test programme came to an end in 2006 and both the ship, and its barge are to be offered up for public display. Both vessels were moved to the Suisun Bay Reserve Anchorage in 2006.

USS Constitution

HISTORIC FLAGSHIP

Ship	Completion Date	Builder
CONSTITUTION	1797	Edmond Hartt's Shipyard, Boston

Propulsion 42,710 sq. ft of sail on three masts **Displacement** 2,200 tonnes **Dimensions** 62m (53m at waterline) x 13.3m x 4.4m **Speed** 13+ knots **Complement** 450 including 55 Marines and 30 boys (1797)

Notes
USS CONSTITUTION is a fully-commissioned US Naval vessel, and is the oldest commissioned warship afloat in the world. Although she is duly recognised and honoured, she holds no official 'flagship' status, though the term is frequently used honourarily. Today she acts in the capacity of the USN's ambassador to the public. Based at Boston, the ship has about 55 active-duty USN crewmembers. About 25 Navy-employed civilians (the Naval Historical Centre, Detachment Boston) perform the in-depth and ongoing maintenance of the ship. Her last major restoration period was in the early 1990's in preparation for the '97 Sail,' the first time she sailed under her own sail power in 116 years. Each year she is taken out into the bay and turned to prevent her masts warping in the prevailing weather.

MILITARY SEALIFT COMMAND

During World War II, four separate government agencies controlled sea transportation. In 1949, the Military Sea Transportation Service, renamed Military Sealift Command (MSC) in 1970, became the single managing agency for the Department of Defence's ocean transportation needs.

From that day on MSC has provided ocean transportation of equipment, fuel, supplies and ammunition to sustain US forces worldwide during peacetime and in war. During a war, more than 95 percent of all equipment and supplies needed by US military forces overseas would be carried by sea.

MSC operates more than 120 ships worldwide on a day-to-day basis and, if needed, has access to more than 100 ships usually kept in a reduced operating status in US ports.

Today, MSC has more than 10,800 employees worldwide, approximately 80 percent of which serve at sea. MSC is the largest employer of merchant mariners in the United States. Approximately 5,100 employees are federal civil service, 660 are military personnel; and another 4,600 are employed by MSC contractors. All MSC ships, unlike other US Navy ships, are crewed by civilians. Some ships have small military departments assigned to carry out communication, supply and aviation functions.

The MSC is organised around four core programmes.

NAVAL FLEET AUXILIARY FORCE PROGRAMME

The Naval Fleet Auxiliary Force provides the bulk of the USN's combat logistics services, the equivalent to the British Royal Fleet Auxiliary. MSC has 36 NFAF ships, that are government-owned vessels, but crewed by civil service mariners - many of the ships were previously USN manned and operated, but have been transferred to MSC operation with considerable operational cost savings. Small Navy departments that previously handled communications and signaling have been replaced by civilian mariners. A similar programme will replace some Navy supply personnel with civilians aboard MSC's five combat stores ships. The NFAF comprises Combat Support ships, Fleet Replenishment oilers, Combat Stores ships and Ammunition ships. Providing fuel, food, ammunition, spare parts and other supplies, NFAF ships enable the USN fleet to remain at sea, on station and combat ready. In addition to delivering supplies at sea, NFAF also operate salvage ships and Fleet tugs for towing and salvage operations. The two Hospital Ships, MERCY and COMFORT are also operated under the NFAF programme.

SPECIAL MISSION PROGRAMME

The Special Mission Programme provides unique vessels and services for a variety of US military and federal government missions. Specialized services include oceanographic and hydrographic surveys, underwater surveillance, missile tracking, acoustic surveys and submarine support.

MSC's Special Mission Programme controls 24 ships supporting several different USN customers, including the Naval Sea Systems Command and the Oceanographer of the Navy. Both civil service and contractor-employed mariners operate these vessels. Technical work, survey operations and communications are conducted by embarked military personnel, civilian scientists and related technicians. Special mission ships average 25 days at sea and five days in port each month.

Oceanographic survey ships study the world's oceans using multi-beam, wide-angle, precision hydrographic sonar systems to collect bathymetric data. One coastal survey ship, USNS JOHN McDONNELL, surveys the sea bottom and collects data in the littoral areas along coastlines. Information gathered is used to develop accurate maritime charts.

Four of the five ocean surveillance ships work directly with the Navy's fleets, listening for undersea threats.

MSC operates one cable-laying ship which transports, deploys, retrieves and repairs submarine cables. ZEUS was built specifically for the Navy; the ship can lay up to 1,000 miles of cable in depths of 9,000 feet during a single deployment before having to restock its cable supply.

Missile range instrumentation ships provide platforms for monitoring missile launches and collecting data which can be used to improve missile efficiency and accuracy. OBSERVATION ISLAND monitors compliance with strategic arms treaties and supports US military weapons test programmes. Other ships provide communication, flight safety, photographic coverage and missile tracking capabilities in support of fleet ballistic missile flight tests.

In addition to its government-owned ships, the Special Mission Programme is responsible for six chartered vessels used for deep water search and rescue missions, Navy submarine test support escorts and Navy and Marine Corps warfare development.

PREPOSITIONING PROGRAMME

The Prepositioning Programme strategically places military equipment and supplies aboard ships in key ocean areas for the US Army, Marine Corps, Air Force, Defence Logistics Agency and Navy. Prepositioning ships remain at sea, ready on short notice to deliver vital equipment, fuel and supplies to support US military forces in the event of a major theatre war, humanitarian operation or other contingency. MSC prepositioning ships are located in three strategic areas: the Mediterranean and eastern Atlantic Ocean, the Indian Ocean and the western Pacific Ocean. The Prepositioning Programme consists of 34 at-sea ships plus 2 aviation support ships kept in reduced operating status. They include long-term chartered commercial vessels, activated Ready Reserve Force ships, and US government-owned ships. All are crewed by mariners provided by companies under contract to MSC.

The Prepositioning Programme is divided into three separate elements: the Combat Prepositioning Force, the Maritime Prepositioning Force and the Logistics Prepositioning ships serving the US Navy, Air Force and Marine Corps and the Defence Logistics Agency.

The Combat Prepositioning Force supports the Army Prepositioned Stocks. Currently, ten ships (eight large, medium speed Ro/Ro vessels and two other vessels) provide quick-response delivery of Army equipment for ground forces.

Sixteen MSC prepositioning ships make up the Maritime Prepositioning Force and are specially configured to transport supplies for the US Marine Corps.

The ships are organized into three squadrons: MPS Squadron One, usually located in the Mediterranean and eastern Atlantic; MPS Squadron Two, usually located at Diego Garcia in the indian Ocean; and MPS Squadron Three, normally in the Guam/Saipan area.

Each squadron carries sufficient equipment and supplies to sustain about 15,000 Marine Corps Air Ground Task Force personnel for up to 30 days. Each ship can discharge cargo either alongside or while anchored offshore using barges carried aboard.

The Logistics Prepositioning Force operates ten vessels for the USN, the Defence

Logistics Agency and the US Air Force.

The Air Force prepositioned fleet consists of munitions carriers such as MV CAPT STEVEN L. BENNETT, MV TSGT JOHN A. CHAPMAN, MV MAJ BERNARD F FISHER and MV A1C WILLIAM H PITSENBARGER.

For Navy prepositioning, MSC operates modular cargo delivery system (MCDS) vessels like SS CAPE JACOB. The vessels carry naval ordnance and also have the capability to operate as shuttle replenishment ships for naval battle groups.

The DLA prepositioning assests include two offshore petroleum distribution system (OPDS) tankers, SS CHESAPEAKE and SS PETERSBURG. The ships carry defence fuel for contingency use.

SEALIFT PROGRAMME

The Sealift Programme provides ocean transportation for the Department of Defence and other government agencies using commercially chartered and government-owned dry cargo ships and tankers. Sealift ships carry DoD cargo to ports not served by regularly scheduled US commercial ocean going vessels. MSC also has access to the US Maritime Administration's Ready Reserve Force.

The Sealift Programme comprises, Tanker, Dry Cargo and Surge Project Offices each ensuring availabilty of suitable shipping.

The heart of the MSC tanker fleet are four Champion-class, double-hulled, ice-strengthened tankers built in 1985. These tankers are government owned and contract operated.

The Dry Cargo Project Office handles all Department of Defence cargo requirements that cannot be accommodated by regularly scheduled ocean liner service. Nearly all peacetime DoD cargo is shipped via US flagged contracted or government-owned ships. During a military contingency, additional vessels may be chartered to expand sealift capabilities to meet additional demand.

The Surge Project Office manages strategic sealift ships that can be activated from reduced operating status to support the US military in exercises, contingencies and war.

MSC's large, medium-speed, roll-on/roll-off ships, or LMSRs, are among the largest cargo ships in the world and can carry up to 380,000 square feet of combat cargo - the equivalent of more than six football fields of wheeled and tracked vehicles - at speeds up to 24 knots. LMSRs are equipped with on board ramps and cranes to assist in loading oversize cargo including helicopters, M1A1 tanks and Bradley armoured personnel carriers. MSC operates eleven surge LMSRs using commercial operating companies to crew and maintain the ships as necessary in order to be ready to sail within 96 hours of notification.

Fast sealift ships are the fastest cargo ships in the world. With speeds in excess of 30 knots, these ships can sail from the US East Coast to Europe in less than six days and to the Gulf in 18 days, ensuring the rapid delivery of needed equipment and supplies. Together, MSC's eight fast sealift ships can deliver nearly all the equipment needed to outfit a full US Army mechanized division.

Ready Reserve Force ships are owned and maintained by the US Department of Transportation's Maritime Administration (MARAD) at strategic locations around the US coasts near Army loading ports. Normally kept in four-, five-, 10- or 20-day reduced operating status, the 59 militarily useful ships come under MSC control when activated. Ships may be activated for humanitarian operations, military exercises and contingencies and for war. The RRF includes tankers, crane ships, roll-on/roll-off ships, heavy lift ships, lighter-aboard-ship vessels and modular cargo delivery system ships. During Operation Iraqi Freedom thirty-three RRF ships were directly involved, delivering more than nine million square feet of combat cargo for US forces in Iraq. RRF ships can be recognised by red, white and blue stripes around their funnel.

SHIPS OF THE MILITARY SEALIFT COMMAND
Pennant Numbers

Ship Number	Pennant	Ship	Pennant Number
NAVAL FLEET AUXILIARY FORCE		PECOS	T-AO 197
		BIG HORN	T-AO 198
		TIPPECANOE	T-AO 199
Ammunition Ships		GUADALUPE	T-AO 200
		PATUXENT	T-AO 201
KILAUEA	T-AE 26	YUKON	T-AO 202
FLINT	T-AE 32	LARAMIE	T-AO 203
SHASTA	T-AE 33	RAPPAHANNOCK	T-AO 204
MOUNT BAKER	T-AE 34		
KISKA	T-AE 35	**Dry Cargo/Ammunition Ships**	
Combat Stores Ships		LEWIS AND CLARK	T-AKE 1
		SACAGAWEA	T-AKE 2
NIAGARA FALLS	T-AFS 3	ALAN SHEPARD	T-AKE 3
CONCORD	T-AFS 5	RICHARD E. BYRD	T-AKE 4
SAN JOSE	T-AFS 7	ROBERT E. PEARY	T-AKE 5
SPICA	T-AFS 9		
SATURN	T-AFS 10	**Hospital Ships**	
Fast Combat Support Ships		MERCY	T-AH 19
		COMFORT	T-AH 20
SUPPLY	T-AOE 6		
RAINIER	T-AOE 7	**Rescue-Salvage Ships**	
ARCTIC	T-AOE 8		
BRIDGE	T-AOE 10	GRASP	T-ARS 51
		SALVOR	T-ARS 52
Fleet Replenishment Oilers		GRAPPLE	T-ARS 53
HENRY J. KAISER	T-AO 187	**Fleet Ocean Tugs**	
JOSHUA HUMPHREYS	T-AO 188		
JOHN LENTHALL	T-AO 189	CATAWBA	T-ATF 168
WALTER S. DIEHL	T-AO 193	NAVAJO	T-ATF 169
JOHN ERICSSON	T-AO 194	SIOUX	T-ATF 171
LEROY GRUMMAN	T-AO 195	APACHE	T-ATF 172
KANAWHA	T-AO 196		

Ship	Pennant Number	Ship	Pennant Number
SPECIAL MISSION SHIPS		**Cable Repair Ship**	
Acoustic Survey Ship		ZEUS	T-ARC 7
HAYES	T-AGOR 195	**Submarine Support Vessels**	
Command Ship		SSV C-COMMANDO	
		MV CAROLYN CHOUEST	
CORONADO	T-AGF 11	MV DOLORES CHOUEST	
Missile Range Instrumentation Ships		MV KELLIE CHOUEST	
		SEALIFT SHIPS	
OBSERVATION ISLAND	T-AGM 23	**Fast Sealift Ships**	
INVINCIBLE	T-AGM 24		
		ALGOL	T-AKR 287
Ocean Surveillance Ships		BELLATRIX	T-AKR 288
		DENEBOLA	T-AKR 289
VICTORIOUS	T-AGOS 19	POLLUX	T-AKR 290
EFFECTIVE	T-AGOS 21	ALTAIR	T-AKR 291
LOYAL	T-AGOS 22	REGULUS	T-AKR 292
IMPECCABLE	T-AGOS 23	CAPELLA	T-AKR 293
		ANTARES	T-AKR 294
Oceanographic Survey Ships		**LMSRs**	
JOHN MCDONNELL	T-AGS 51		
PATHFINDER	T-AGS 60	SHUGHART	T-AKR 295
SUMNER	T-AGS 61	GORDON	T-AKR 296
BOWDITCH	T-AGS 62	YANO	T-AKR 297
HENSON	T-AGS 63	GILLILAND	T-AKR 298
BRUCE C. HEEZEN	T-AGS 64	BOB HOPE	T-AKR 300
MARY SEARS	T-AGS 65	FISHER	T-AKR 301
		SEAY	T-AKR 302
Navigation Test Support Ship		MENDONCA	T-AKR 303
		PILILAAU	T-AKR 304
WATERS	T-AGS 45	BRITTIN	T-AKR 305
		BENAVIDEZ	T-AKR 306

Ship	Pennant Number	Ship	Pennant Number
Government-owned Tankers		SSG EDWARD A. CARTER	T-AK 4544
PAUL BUCK	T-AOT 1122	A1C WILLIAM H PITSENBARGER	T-AK 4638
SAMUEL L. COBB	T-AOT 1123		
RICHARD G. MATTHIESEN	T-AOT 1124	**Container & Roll-on/Roll-off Ships**	
LAWRENCE H. GIANELLA	T-AOT 1125	TSGT JOHN A. CHAPMAN	T-AK 323
Container Ship		CPL LOUIS J. HAUGE JR.	T-AK 3000
MV BAFFIN STRAIT	T-AK W9519	PFC WILLIAM B. BAUGH	T-AK 3001
Long-term Chartered Tanker		PFC JAMES ANDERSON JR.	T-AK 3002
MT MONTAUK		1ST LT ALEX BONNYMAN	T-AK 3003
		PVT FRANKLIN J. PHILLIPS	T-AK 3004
PREPOSITIONING SHIPS		SGT MATEJ KOCAK	T-AK 3005
LMSRs		PFC EUGENE A. OBREGON	T-AK 3006
WATSON	T-AKR 310	MAJ STEPHEN W. PLESS	T-AK 3007
SISLER	T-AKR 311	2ND LT JOHN P. BOBO	T-AK 3008
DAHL	T-AKR 312	PFC DEWAYNE T. WILLIAMS	T-AK 3009
RED CLOUD	T-AKR 313	1ST LT BALDOMERO LOPEZ	T-AK 3010
CHARLTON	T-AKR 314	1ST LT JACK LUMMUS	T-AK 3011
WATKINS	T-AKR 315	SGT WILLIAM R. BUTTON	T-AK 3012
POMEROY	T-AKR 316	1ST LT HARRY L. MARTIN	T-AK 3015
SODERMAN	T-AKR 317	LCPL ROY M. WHEAT	T-AK 3016
Container Ships			
CAPT STEVEN L. BENNETT	T-AK 4296		
MAJ BERNARD F FISHER	T-AK 4396		
LTC JOHN U. D. PAGE	T-AK 4496		

Ship	Pennant Number	Ship	Pennant Number
GYSGT FRED W. STOCKHAM	T-AK 3017	CAPE TAYLOR	T-AKR 113
		ADM WM. M. CALLAGHAN	T-AKR 1001
Government owned Tankers		CAPE ORLANDO	T-AKR 2044
		CAPE DUCATO	T-AKR 5051
CHESAPEAKE	T-AOT 5084	CAPE DOUGLAS	T-AKR 5052
PETERSBURG	T-AOT 9101	CAPE DOMINGO	T-AKR 5053
		CAPE DECISION	T-AKR 5054
Aviation Maintenance Logistics Ships		CAPE DIAMOND	T-AKR 5055
		CAPE ISABEL	T-AKR 5062
		CAPE HUDSON	T-AKR 5066
WRIGHT	T-AVB 3	CAPE HENRY	T-AKR 5067
CURTISS	T-AVB 4	CAPE HORN	T-AKR 5068
		CAPE EDMONT	T-AKR 5069
		CAPE INSCRIPTION	T-AKR 5076
READY RESERVE FORCE SHIPS		CAPE LAMBERT	T-AKR 5077
		CAPE LOBOS	T-AKR 5078
Modular Cargo Delivery System Ships		CAPE KNOX	T-AKR 5082
		CAPE KENNEDY	T-AKR 5083
		CAPE VINCENT	T-AKR 9666
CAPE GIRARDEAU	T-AK 2039	CAPE RISE	T-AKR 9678
CAPE JACOB	T-AK 5029	CAPE RAY	T-AKR 9679
CAPE GIBSON	T-AK 5051	CAPE VICTORY	T-AKR 9701
		CAPE TRINITY	T-AKR 9711
Lighter Aboard Ships		CAPE RACE	T-AKR 9960
		CAPE WASHINGTON	T-AKR 9961
CAPE FEAR	T-AK 5061	CAPE WRATH	T-AKR 9962
CAPE FLATTERY	T-AK 5070		
CAPE FLORIDA	T-AK 5071	**Heavy Lift Ships**	
CAPE FAREWELL	T-AK 5073		
		CAPE MAY	T-AKR 5063
Roll-on/Roll-off Ships		CAPE MOHICAN	T-AKR 5065
COMET	T-AKR 7	**Government-owned Tankers**	
METEOR	T-AKR 9		
CAPE ISLAND	T-AKR 10	NODAWAY	T-AOT 78
CAPE INTREPID	T-AKR 11	ALATNA	T-AOT 81
CAPE TEXAS	T-AKR 112	CHATTAHOOCHEE	T-AOT 82

Ship	Pennant Number	Ship	Pennant Number
Crane Ships		DIAMOND STATE	T-ACS 7
		EQUALITY STATE	T-ACS 8
KEYSTONE STATE	T-ACS 1	GREEN MOUNTAIN STATE	
GEM STATE	T-ACS 2		T-ACS 9
GRAND CANYON STATE		BEAVER STATE	T-ACS 10
	T-ACS 3		
GOPHER STATE	T-ACS 4	**High-Speed Vessel**	
FLICKERTAIL STATE	T-ACS 5		
CORNHUSKER STATE	T-ACS 6	WESTPAC EXPRESS	HSV 4676

US NAVY/PH JASON D. LANDON

AMMUNITION SHIPS
KILAUEA CLASS

Ship	Pennant Number	Completion Date	Builder
KILAUEA	T-AE 26	1968	GD, Quincy
FLINT	T-AE 32	1971	Ingalls
SHASTA	T-AE 33	1972	Ingalls
MOUNT BAKER	T-AE 34	1972	Ingalls
KISKA	T-AE 35	1972	Ingalls

Machinery 3 Foster-Wheeler boilers; 1 GE turbine driving 1 shaft **Displacement** 19,940 tonnes (Full Load) **Dimensions** 171.9 x 24.7 x 8.5m **Speed** 20 knots **Armament** None **Aircraft** 2 x CH-46E Sea Knight or CH-60 Seahawks **Complement** 125-133 civilian (plus 7-24 military)

Notes
Former USN ships transferred to the MSC (KILAUEA 1980, FLINT 1995, KISKA and MOUNT BAKER 1996 and SHASTA 1997). They provide underway replenishment of all types of ammunition via heavy jackstay and vertical replenishment. KILAUEA is in reduced operating status.

USNS San Jose

COMBAT STORES SHIPS
MARS CLASS

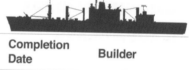

Ship	Pennant Number	Completion Date	Builder
NIAGARA FALLS	T-AFS 3	1967	NASSCo
CONCORD	T-AFS 5	1968	NASSCo
SAN JOSE	T-AFS 7	1970	NASSCo

Machinery 3 Babcock & Wilcox boilers; 1 De Laval turbine driving one shaft; 22,000shp **Displacement** 18,962 tonnes **Dimensions** 177.1m x 24.1m x 7.3m **Speed** 21knots Aircraft 2 x CH-46 Sea Knight or civilian equivalent **Complement** 136 Civilian (plus 26 miltary).

Notes
Former USN ships transferred to the MSC (CONCORD 1992, SAN JOSE 1993 and NIAGARA FALLS 1994). These ships provide underway replenishment of all types of supplies including fresh, frozen and chilled food; dry provisions; spare parts; clothing; and mail using tensioned cargo rigs and helicopters.

USNS Spica

SIRIUS CLASS

Ship	Pennant Number	Completion Date	Builder
SPICA	T-AFS 9	1968	Swan Hunter
SATURN	T-AFS 10	1967	Swan Hunter

Machinery One Wallsend-Sulzer 8RD76 diesel driving one shaft **Displacement** 17,061 tonnes **Dimensions** 159.7m x 22m x 6.7m **Speed** 19 knots   **Aircraft** 2 x Super Puma **Complement** 103 civilian (plus 26 military).

Notes

SIRIUS (ex LYNESS) was transferred from the UK Royal Fleet Auxiliary to MSC in 1981, SPICA (ex TARBATNESS) in 1981, and SATURN (ex STROMNESS) in 1983. In US service the ships were fitted with a hangar. They operate two commercially chartered Super Puma helicopters for vertical replenishment.   SIRIUS was decommissioned in 2005 and transferred to the Texas Maritime Academy, where she became their new training ship, TEXAS CLIPPER III.

USNS Ranier

FAST COMBAT SUPPORT SHIPS

SUPPLY CLASS

Ship	Pennant Number	Completion Date	Builder
SUPPLY	T-AOE 6	1994	NASSCo SD
RAINIER	T-AOE 7	1995	NASSCo SD
ARCTIC	T-AOE 8	1995	NASSCo SD
BRIDGE	T-AOE 10	1997	NASSCo SD

Machinery Four GE LM2500 gas-turbines driving two shafts; 105,000shp **Displacement** 49,583 tonnes **Dimensions** 229.9m x 32m x 11.6m **Speed** 25 knots **Aircraft** 3 x CH-46E Sea Knight helicopters **Complement** 160 civilians (59 military)

Notes

Transferred from the USN between 2001-04, these high speed vessels are the largest combat logistics ships in the MSC. These ships have the speed to keep up with the carrier groups and are able to resupply fuel, lubricants, dry stores and ammunition.

USNS Tippecanoe

FLEET REPLENISHMENT OILER

HENRY J. KAISER CLASS

Ship	Pennant Number	Completion Date	Builder
HENRY J. KAISER	T-AO 187	1986	Avondale
JOHN LENTHALL	T-AO 189	1987	Avondale
WALTER S DIEHL	T-AO 193	1988	Avondale
JOHN ERICSSON	T-AO 194	1991	Avondale
LEROY GRUMMAN	T-AO 195	1989	Avondale
KANAWHA	T-AO 196	1991	Avondale
PECOS	T-AO 197	1990	Avondale
BIG HORN	T-AO 198	1992	Avondale
TIPPECANOE	T-AO 199	1993	Avondale
GUADALUPE	T-AO 200	1992	Avondale

Ship	Pennant Number	Completion Date	Builder
PATUXENT	T-AO 201	1995	Avondale
YUKON	T-AO 202	1993	Avondale
LARAMIE	T-AO 203	1996	Avondale
RAPPAHANNOCK	T-AO 204	1995	Avondale

Machinery 2 Colt-Pielstick 10 PC4.2 V 570 diesels driving 2 shafts; Controllable Pitch propellors **Displacement** 42,674 tonnes **Dimensions** 206.5m x 29.7m x 4m **Speed** 20 knots **Complement** 66-89 civilian (7-24 military)

Notes

Fitted with medium-speed diesel propulsion, the delivery of PATUXENT, RAPPAHANNOCK and LARAMIE were delayed by the decision to fit double hulls to meet the requirements of the Oil Pollution Act of 1990. This modification increased construction time from 32 to 42 months and reduced cargo capacity by 17 percent, although this can be restored in an emergency. Hull separation is 1.83 m at the sides and 1.98 m on the bottom. HENRY J. KAISER and JOSHUA HUMPHREYS are in reduced operating status.

•NASSCO   **USNS Lewis and Clark**

AUXILIARY DRY CARGO SHIPS
LEWIS AND CLARK CLASS

Ship	Pennant Number	Completion Date	Builder
LEWIS AND CLARK	T-AKE 1	2006	GD NASSCo
SACAGAWEA	T-AKE 2	*2007*	GD NASSCo
ALAN SHEPARD	T-AKE 3	*2007*	GD NASSCo
RICHARD E. BYRD	T-AKE 4	*2007*	GD NASSCo
ROBERT E. PEARY	T-AKE 5	*2008*	GD NASSCo

Machinery Integrated propulsion and ship service electrical distribution system; Four FM/MAN diesel generators with total installed power of 35.7 MW. Twin synchronous, variable speed, reversible, double-wound, Alstom propulsion motors mounted in tandem, Single fixed-pitch propeller **Displacement** 40,945 tons **Dimensions** 210m x 32.31m x 9m **Speed** 20 knots **Complement** 123 civilian (plus 49 military)

Notes

This class will replace the current Kilauea-class ammunition ships, Mars and Sirius-class combat stores ships, and when operating in concert with a Henry J. Kaiser-class (T-AO 187) oiler, they will replace the Sacramento-class (AOE) fast combat support ship. The T-AKE Programme will consist of 11 ships with a budget of approximately $4 billion. LEWIS AND CLARK was delivered on 20 June 2006.

USNS Mercy

HOSPITAL SHIPS
MERCY CLASS

Ship	Pennant Number	Completion Date	Conversion
MERCY	T-AH 19	1986	NASSCo SD
COMFORT	T-AH 20	1987	NASSCo SD

Machinery 2 GE turbines; two boilers; one shaft **Displacement** 70,473 tonnes **Dimensions** 272.6m x 32.2m x 10m **Speed** 17.5 knots **Complement** 63 (plus 956 Naval medical staff and 258 Naval support staff).

Notes

Both ships are converted San Clemente-class super tankers. MERCY was delivered in 1986 and COMFORT in 1987. Normally, the ships are kept in a reduced operating status, one at Baltimore and the other at San Diego. The ships can be fully activated and crewed within five days.Each ship contains 12 fully-equipped operating rooms, a 1,000 bed hospital facility, digital radiological services, a medical laboratory, a pharmacy, an optometry lab, a CAT-scan and two oxygen producing plants. Each ship is equipped with a helicopter deck capable of landing large military helicopters. The ships also have side ports to take on patients at sea. MERCY was fitted with a temporary hangar structure in 2006.

• US NAVY/PH1 ARLO K. ABRAHAMSON — **USNS Catawba**

FLEET OCEAN TUGS
POWHATAN CLASS

Ship	Pennant Number	Completion Date	Builder
CATAWBA	T-ATF 168	1980	Marinette Marine
NAVAJO	T-ATF 169	1980	Marinette Marine
SIOUX	T-ATF 171	1981	Marinette Marine
APACHE	T-ATF 172	1981	Marinette Marine

Machinery 2 GM EMD 20-645F7B diesels driving 2 shafts; Kort nozzles; controllable pitch props; bow thruster **Displacement** 2,296.27 tonnes **Dimensions** 73.2m x 12.8m x 4.6m **Speed** 14.5 knots **Complement** 16 civilians (four naval communicators)

Notes

Fleet tugs are used to tow ships, barges and targets for gunnery exercises. They are also used as platforms for salvage and diving work, as participants in naval exercises, to conduct search and rescue missions, to aid in the clean up of oil spills and ocean accidents, and to provide fire fighting assistance. Each vessel is equipped with a 10 ton capacity crane and have a bollard pull of at least 87 tons. There are two GPH fire pumps supplying three fire monitors able to produce up to 2,200 gallons of foam per minute. Can operate as platforms for Navy divers in the recovery of downed aircraft or sunken ships.

USNS Grasp

RESCUE AND SALVAGE VESSEL
SAFEGUARD CLASS

Ship	Pennant Number	Completion Date	Builder
GRASP	T-ARS 51	1985	Peterson
SALVOR	T-ARS 52	1986	Peterson
GRAPPLE	T-ARS 53	1985	Peterson

Machinery Four Caterpiller 399 Diesels, two shafts, 4,200 horsepower **Displacement** 3,200 tons **Dimensions** 77.7m x 15.2m x 4.7m **Speed** 15 knots **Complement** 26 (plus 4 US Navy)

Notes
Transferred to MSC in January 2006 (GRASP); July 2006 (GRAPPLE) and January 2007 (SALVOR). The rugged construction of these steel-hulled ships, combined with speed and endurance, make these rescue and salvage ships well-suited for rescue/salvage operations of Navy and commercial shipping throughout the world.

USNS Hayes

ACOUSTIC SURVEY SHIP

Ship	Pennant Number	Completion Date	Builder
HAYES	T-AGOR 16	1971	Todd SY, Seattle

Machinery Diesel-electric; 2 Caterpiller diesels, 2 generators, 2 Westinghouse motors, 2,400 hp; 2 auxiliary diesels (for creep speed); 330 hp; 2 shafts, controllable pitch props **Displacement** 4,015 tonnes **Dimensions** 78.2m x 22.9m x 6.7m **Speed** 10 knots **Complement** 19 civilian mariners, 7 Naval personnel and 30 scientists.

Notes

In 1984 she was transferred to the Maritime Administration at James River for lay-up. Under the FY86 programme, she was converted to an Acoustic Research Ship and reclassified T-AG 195. The conversion was completed in early 1992 after five years' work in two shipyards. The ships mission is to transport, deploy and retrieve acoustic arrays, to conduct acoustic surveys in support of the submarine noise reduction programme and to perform acoustic testing. The catamaran design provides a stable platform with a large deck availability.

CABLE REPAIR SHIP

Ship	Pennant Number	Completion Date	Builder
ZEUS	T-ARC 7	1984	NASSCo SD

Machinery Diesel-electric, twin shaft, 10,200shp **Displacement** 14,384.19 tonnes **Dimensions** 153.2m x 22.3m x 7.6m **Speed** 15 knots **Complement** 51 civilians, 6 military and 32 scientists

Notes

ZEUS is the first multi-mission cable ship designed and built by the US Navy from the keel up. Its two main missions are oceanographic survey and the installation and maintenance of submarine cable systems.

MISSILE RANGE
INSTRUMENTATION SHIPS

Ship	Pennant Number	Completion Date	Builder
OBSERVATION ISLAND	T-AGM 23	1953	New York SB, Camden

Machinery Two boilers; 1 GE turbine driving one shaft; 19,250shp **Displacement** 17,288.06 tonnes (FL) **Dimensions** 171.6m x 23.2m x 7.6m **Speed** 20 knots **Complement** 66 civilians, 59 technicians

Notes

OBSERVATION ISLAND was built as a Mariner class merchant ship. She was acquired by the USN in 1956 for use as a Fleet Ballistic Missile test ship. The vessel was converted at Norfolk Naval Shipyard bur placed in reserve in 1972. She was brought froward from reserve in 1977 transferring to MSC as T-AGM 23. She operates worldwide, monitoring compliance with strategic arms treaties and supporting US military weapons test programmes.

In 2006 VT Halter Marine Inc. was awarded a design and construction contract for a T-AGM (R) Cobra Judy replacement ship. Construction is scheduled to begin in 2008, with delivery in 2010.

INVINCIBLE CLASS

Ship	Pennant Number	Completion Date	Builder
INVINCIBLE	T-AGM 24	1987	Tacoma Boat

Machinery Four diesel generators driving two shafts; 1,600 shp **Displacement** 2,262 tonnes (FL) **Dimensions** 68.3m x 13.1m x 4.5m **Speed** 11 knots **Complement** 18 Civilian; 18 Military

Notes

A converted Stalwart-class T-AGOS vessel, she provides a platform for a dual-band radar developed by the US Air Force to support its collection requirements against theatre ballistic missiles. She assumed her new role in 2000.

USNS John McDonnell

OCEANOGRAPHIC SURVEY SHIPS

Ship	Pennant Number	Completion Date	Builder
JOHN McDONNELL	T-AGS 51	1991	Halter Marine

Machinery One GM EMD diesel driving one shaft **Displacement** 2,054 tonnes (FL)
Dimensions 63.4m x 13.7m x 4.3m **Speed** 12 knots **Complement** 22 plus 11 scientists

Notes

Designed for coastal surveying she carries 34-foot survey launches for data collection in coastal regions with depths between 10 and 600 m and in deep water to 4,000 m. A small diesel is used for propulsion at towing speeds of up to 6 knots. SIMRAD high-frequency active hull-mounted and side scan sonars are carried.

USNS Bruce C. Heezen

PATHFINDER CLASS

Ship	Pennant Number	Completion Date	Builder
PATHFINDER	T-AGS 60	1994	Freide-Goldman-Halter
SUMNER	T-AGS 61	1995	Freide-Goldman-Halter
BOWDITCH	T-AGS 62	1996	Freide-Goldman-Halter
HENSON	T-AGS 63	1998	Freide-Goldman-Halter
BRUCE C. HEEZEN	T-AGS 64	2000	Freide-Goldman-Halter
MARY SEARS	T-AGS 65	2001	Freide-Goldman-Halter

Machinery Diesel-electric; 4 EMD/Baylor diesel generators; 2 GE CDF 1944 motors **Displacement** 4,762 tonnes (FL) **Dimensions** 100.1m x 17.7m x 5.8m **Speed** 16 knots **Complement** 25 plus 27 scientists

Notes

The contract for this class was awarded in January 1991. They are equipped with three multipurpose cranes and five winches together with a variety of oceanographic equipment including multibeam echo-sounders, towed sonars and expendable sensors.

USNS Waters

WATERS CLASS

Ship	Pennant Number	Completion Date	Builder
WATERS	T-AGS 45	1993	NG Avondale

Machinery Diesel-electric, twin-screw; 7,400shp **Displacement** 12,403 tonnes (FL) **Dimensions** 139.3m x 21m x 6.4m **Speed** 13 knots **Complement** 32 civilians and 59 technicians

Notes

WATERS was delivered in 1993 as an oceanographic survey ship. She was converted in 1998 under the sponsorship of the Strategic Systems Programme Office. She began operations in 1999, replacing VANGUARD (deactivated in 1998) and RANGE SENTINEL (deactivated in 1997). WATERS supports submarine navigation system testing and provides ballistic missile flight test support services.

OCEAN SURVEILLANCE SHIPS

VICTORIOUS CLASS

Ship	Pennant Number	Completion Date	Builder
VICTORIOUS	T-AGOS 19	1991	McDermott Inc
EFFECTIVE	T-AGOS 21	1993	McDermott Inc
LOYAL	T-AGOS 22	1993	McDermott Inc

Machinery Diesel-electric; 4 Caterpillar diesel generators, 2 GE motors, twin screw 1,600shp; 2 bow thrusters **Displacement** 3,396 tonnes (FL) **Dimensions** 71.5m x 28.5m x 7.6m **Speed** 16 knots **Complement** 38

Notes

Ships are built on a Small Waterplane Twin Hull, or SWATH, design for greater stability at slow speeds in high latitudes under adverse weather conditions. Ocean surveillance ships have a single mission to gather underwater acoustical data. The T-AGOS ships operate to support the anti-submarine warfare mission of the commanders of the Atlantic and Pacific Fleets. They use surveillance towed-array sensor system (SURTASS) equipment to gather undersea acoustic data. The ships also carry electronic equipment to process and transmit that data via satellite to shore stations for evaluation.

IMPECCABLE CLASS

Ship	Pennant Number	Completion Date	Builder
IMPECCABLE	T-AGOS 23	2001	Tamp SY/Halter Marine

Machinery Diesel-electric; three diesel generators; 2 Westinghouse motors driving twin screw shaft; 2 omni-thruster hydrojets **Displacement** 5,370 tonnes (FL) **Dimensions** 85.8m x 29.2m x 7.9m **Speed** 12 knots **Complement** 26 Civilian; 19 Military

Notes

The keel for IMPECCABLE was laid down on 2 February 1993. The ship was more than 60 percent complete when the shipyard encountered difficulties. The contract was sub-let to Halter Marine on 20 April 1995 to complete the ship. IMPECCABLE finally entered MSC service in October 2001. the ship has a hull form based on that of the Victorious class, but has a more powerful propulsion plant and is designed specifically for deploying an additional active towed-array system.

MV Cory Chouest

OCEAN SURVEILLANCE SHIP

Ship	Pennant Number	Completion Date	Builder
CORY CHOUEST		1974	Ulstein Hatlo, Norway

Machinery Two diesels driving two shafts **Displacement** 3,900 tonnes (FL) **Dimensions** 81.5m x 18.4m x 4.6m **Speed** 11 knots **Complement** 16 plus 41 military/scientists

Notes

The vessel, based at Hawaii, is used as an ocean surveillance ship, serving as the platform for the Surveillance Towed Array Sensor System (SURTASS) and the Low Frequency Array (LFA) programmes. To undertake its new role the vessel had all of the engines and generators remounted for noise reduction and the original cargo and handling deck was equipped with modular laboratories and living facilities for up to 60 scientists. The charter has been extended through to 2008.

Westpac Express

HIGH SPEED VESSELS

Ship	Pennant Number	Completion Date	Builder
WESTPAC EXPRESS		2001	Austal Ships Pty.

Machinery Four Caterpillar 3618 Diesels; Four KaMeWa Waterjets **Displacement** 750 Dwt **Dimensions** 101m x 26.65m x 4.2m **Speed** 36 knots **Complement** 12 Military, 13 Civilian

Notes

Chartered by the MSC since 2001and is used for operations supporting the Third Marine Expeditionary Force (III MEF) of the USMC based at Okinawa. The vessel can rapidly transport a complete battalion of 950 marines together with up to 550 tonnes of vehicles and equipment, in one lift. Using a commercial high speed vessel to transport III MEF personnel and equipment frees about 10 military transport planes and one ship for other military purposes.

SUBMARINE SUPPORT VESSELS

Ship	Pennant Number	Completion Date	Builder
CAROLYN CHOUEST		1994	North American SB
KELLIE CHOUEST		1996	North American SB
DOLORES CHOUEST		1978	North American SB
C-COMMANDO		1997	Leevac Industries

Machinery Two diesels driving two shafts **Displacement** 1,599 tonnes (FL) **Dimensions** 74.3m x 16.3m x 5.3m **Speed** 12 knots **Complement** 15 plus mission crew (All figures for Carolyn Chouest)

Notes
The MSC Special Mission Programme manages the operation of these four chartered ships used for submarine support activities. CAROLYN CHOUEST and DOLORES CHOUEST operate on the east coast, KELLIE CHOUEST operates on the west coast and C COMMANDO is based in Hawaii. CAROLYN CHOUEST is the designated support vessel for Submarine NR-1; DOLORES and KELLIE CHOUEST support the DSRV programme and C-COMMANDO is the designated support ship for the Advanced Seal Delivery System. All except DOLORES CHOUEST are generally similar.

USNS Richard G. Mattheisen

TRANSPORT TANKERS
CHAMPION CLASS

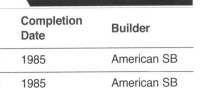

Ship	Pennant Number	Completion Date	Builder
PAUL BUCK	T-AOT 1122	1985	American SB
SAMUEL L. COBB	T-AOT 1123	1985	American SB
RICHARD G. MATTHEISEN	T-AOT 1124	1986	American SB
LAWRENCE H. GIANELLA	T-AOT 1125	1986	American SB

Machinery One Mitsubishi or one Ishikawajima-Sulzer diesel driving one shaft; 15,300shp **Displacement** 39,000 tons approx **Dimensions** 187.5m x 27.4m x 10.4m **Speed** 16 knots **Complement** 31.

Notes
This class was built for long term charter to MSC. All have double hulls and are ice-strengthened for protection against damage during missions in extreme climates. The last two are able to rig replenishment gear. All were purchased by MSC in 2003, making them US Naval Ships. A fifth vessel GUS W. DARNELL was acquired by USA Shipping Partners LP in 2005 and renamed HOUSTON. A further smaller, shallow draft tanker, MT MONTAUK is also on long term charter.

USNS Pollux

FAST SEALIFT SHIPS

Ship	Pennant Number	In Service	Builder
ALGOL	T-AKR 287	1984	Rotterdamse DDM
BELLATRIX	T-AKR 288	1984	Rheinstaht NSW Emden
DENEBOLA	T-AKR 289	1985	Rotterdamse DDM
POLLUX	T-AKR 290	1986	AG Weser Bremen
ALTAIR	T-AKR 291	1985	Rheinstaht NSW Emden
REGULUS	T-AKR 292	1985	AG Weser Bremen
CAPELLA	T-AKR 293	1984	Rotterdamse DMM
ANTARES	T-AKR 294	1984	AG Weser Bremen

Machinery Two GE MST19 geared steam turbines driving two shafts; 120,00shp **Displacement** 55,355 tonnes (FL) **Dimensions** 288.4m x 32.3m x 10.6m **Speed** 33 knots **Complement** 42

Notes
The fastest cargo ships in the world, they can travel at speed of up to 33 knots and are capable of sailing from the US East Coast to Europe in just six days, and to the Persian Gulf via the Suez Canal in 18 days. Combined, all eight ships can carry nearly all the equipment needed to outfit a full Army mechanized division.

USNS Gordon

LARGE, MEDIUM SPEED, RO-RO SHIPS

GORDON CLASS

Ship	Pennant Number	In Service	Builder
GORDON	T-AKR 296	1996	AS Burmeister & Wan Denmark
GILLILAND	T-AKR 298	1997	AS Burmeister & Wan Denmark

Machinery Three Burmeister & Wain diesels driving three shafts; 1 x 31,400shp 2 x 23,600shp **Displacement** 57,000 tons **Dimensions** 272.6m x 32.2m x 11m **Speed** 24 knots **Complement** 45 (+ 50 USN)

Notes

Each ship can carry an entire U.S. Army Task Force, including 58 tanks, 48 other tracked vehicles, plus more than 900 trucks and other wheeled vehicles. Two 110-ton single pedestal twin cranes make it possible to load and unload cargo where shoreside infrastructure is limited or non-existent.

USNS Shughart

SHUGHART CLASS

Ship	Pennant Number	In Service	Builder
SHUGHART	T-AKR 295	1996	Odense Staal A/S Lindo Denmark
YANO	T-AKR 297	1997	Odense Staal A/S Lindo Denmark

Machinery Two Burmeister & Wain diesels driving one shaft; 47,300shp **Displacement** 55,123 tonnes **Dimensions** 276.4m x 32.3m x 10.6m **Speed** 24 knots **Complement** 45 (plus up to 100 USN/USMC)

Notes
Former Mearsk Line container ships built in 1981 and lengthened in 1987 by Hyundai. They were converted by NASSCo in 1993 with a stern slewing ramp, side access hatches and improved cargo handling equipment.

USNS Mendonca

BOB HOPE CLASS

Ship	Pennant Number	Completion Date	Builder
BOB HOPE	T-AKR 300	1998	NG Avondale
FISHER	T-AKR 301	1999	NG Avondale
SEAY	T-AKR 302	2000	NG Avondale
MENDONCA	T-AKR 303	2000	NG Avondale
PILILAAU	T-AKR 304	2001	NG Avondale
BRITTIN	T-AKR 305	2002	NG Avondale
BENAVIDEZ	T-AKR 306	2003	NG Avondale

Machinery Four Colt Pielstick diesels driving two shafts; 65,160shp **Displacement** 62,096 tons **Dimensions** 289.6m x 32.3m x 11.2m **Speed** 24.9 knots **Complement** 27 - accommodation for 95 (plus 300 troops)

Notes
Purpose built LMSRs, rather than merchant ship conversions, these vessels have a cargo carrying capacity of more than 380,000 square feet.

USNS Dahl

WATSON CLASS

Ship	Pennant Number	Completion Date	Builder
WATSON	T-AKR 310	1998	NASSCo
SISLER	T-AKR 311	1998	NASSCo
DAHL	T-AKR 312	1999	NASSCo
RED CLOUD	T-AKR 313	2000	NASSCo
CHARLTON	T-AKR 314	2000	NASSCo
WATKINS	T-AKR 315	2001	NASSCo
POMEROY	T-AKR 316	2001	NASSCo
SODERMAN	T-AKR 317	2002	NASSCo

Machinery Two GE LM2500-30 Gas Turbines driving two shafts; 64,000shp
Displacement 62,700 tons **Dimensions** 289.6m x 32.2m x 12.9m **Speed** 24.9 knots
Complement 30

Notes
The largest gas turbine powered vessels afloat, they were originally to have been 36 knot ships, but costs prevented this.

SS Curtis

AVIATION LOGISTICS SHIPS

Ship	Pennant Number	In Service	Builder
CURTIS	T-AVB 3	1987	Ingalls SB
WRIGHT	T-AVB 4	1986	Ingalls SB

Machinery Two GE geared steam turbines driving one shaft; 30,000shp **Displacement** 12,409 tonnes **Dimensions** 183.5m x 27.43m x 10.36m **Speed** 23 knots **Complement** 33 (plus 300 USMC)

Notes
Primary mission is to support USMC helicopters. Additional accommodation built aft and a flight deck built forward of the derricks. Can accommodate 300 maintenance containers. Vehicles can be offloaded by a stern ramp or side door. Both ships have 10 x 30 ton cranes and a single 70 ton crane for cargo handling. Both ships are operated under contract by Crowley Liner Services. Both vessels are part of the Ready Reserve Force but are dedicated to USMC Aviation Logistics Support under the Prepositioning Programme.

SS Chesapeake (deploying OPDS)

TRANSPORT TANKERS

Ship	Pennant Number	To RRF	Builder
SS PETERSBURG	T-AOT 5075	1991	Bethlehem SY
SS CHESAPEAKE	T-AOT 5084	1991	Bethlehem SY

Machinery Two Bethlehem geared steam turbines driving one shaft **Displacement** 65,000 tonnes **Dimensions** 224.44m x 31.22m x 12.13m **Speed** 14.9 knots **Complement** 34-38

Notes

Built in 1963/64, both vessels carry a barge mounted Offshore Petroleum Discharge System (OPDS) forward of the bridge. The vessels are designed to incline and launch a Single Anchor Leg Moor (SALM). They can deliver petroleum products within 48 hours of arriving on station discharging at a rate of 1.4 million gallons per day up to four miles offshore and at a water depth as shallow as 200 feet. Each is capable of carrying more than 10.7 Million gallons of jet or other fuels as required. Ships are operated under contract by Interocean American Shipping Corporation. Both are part of the Ready Reserve Force, but have been activated for duty with the Prepositioning Programme. Four other smaller Government-owned tankers (POTOMAC; ALATNA; CHATTAHOOCHIE and NODAWAY) are operated as part of the Ready Reserve Force.

MV Pfc William B. Baugh

CONTAINER & RO-RO SHIPS

CPL. LOUIS J. HAUGE JR CLASS

Ship	Pennant Number	In Service	Builder
CPL. LOUIS J. HAUGE JR	T-AK 3000	1984	Odense Staal A/S Lindo
PFC WILLIAM B. BAUGH	T-AK 3001	1984	Odense Staal A/S Lindo
PFC JAMES ANDERSON JR	T-AK 3002	1985	Odense Staal A/S Lindo
1st LT ALEX BONNYMAN	T-AK 3003	1985	Odense Staal A/S Lindo
PVT. FRANKLIN J. PHILLIPS	T-AK 3004	1985	Odense Staal A/S Lindo

Machinery One Sulzer diesel driving one shaft; 16,800shp **Displacement** 49,453 tonnes **Dimensions** 230.25m x 27.48m x 10.02m **Speed** 21 knots **Complement** 20 (plus 7 MSC, 30 maintainers and 80 troops)

Notes
Part of MPS 2 Squadron based at Diego Garcia. Equipped with four 30 ton and two 36 ton pedestal cranes. Side loading vehicle ports and a slewing after ramp aid rapid onload/off load of vehicles from 3 decks.

SGT. MATEJ KOCAK CLASS

Ship	Pennant Number	In Service	Builder
SGT. MATEJ KOCAK	T-AK 3005	1984	Sun SB, Chester PA
PFC EUGENE A. OBREGON	T-AK 3006	1985	Sun SB, Chester PA
MAJ. STEPHEN W. PLESS	T-AK 3007	1985	Sun SB, Chester PA

Displacement 19,588 tons **Dimensions** 250.2m x 32.2m x 5.7m **Speed** 23 knots
Complement 85 (plus 7 MSC, 8 USN and 25 maintainers)

Notes

The second class of MPS ships chartered by MSC, they gained 157 feet amidships and a helicopter landing platform after conversion. These ships, delivered to MSC in the mid-1980s, were converted by NASSCo, San Diego, and owned and operated by Waterman Steamship Corp. Based in the Mediterranean, each ship is intended to carry 25% of the vehicles, fuel and stores required to support a USMC Marine Expeditionary Brigade. Ships have twin 50 ton and 35 ton cranes forward of the bridge and a 30 ton travelling gantry crane.

MV 1st Lt. Jack Lummus

2ND LT. JOHN P. BOBO CLASS

Ship	Pennant Number	In Service	Builder
2nd LT. JOHN P. BOBO	T-AK-3008	1985	GD Quincy, MA
PFC. DEWAYNE T. WILLIAMS	T-AK 3009	1985	GD Quincy, MA
1st LT. BALDOMERO LOPEZ	T-AK 3010	1985	GD Quincy, MA
1st LT. JACK LUMMUS	T-AK 3011	1986	GD Quincy, MA
SGT. WILLIAM R. BUTTON	T-AK 3012	1986	GD Quincy, MA

Machinery Two Stork Werkspoor Diesels driving one shaft; 26,400shp **Displacement** 45,039 tonnes **Dimensions** 205.9m x 32.2m x 9.8m **Speed** 23 knots **Complement** 38 civilians, 10 technicians.

Notes

The 2nd Lt. JOHN P. BOBO Class ships were new construction ships delivered to MSC in the mid-1980s from General Dynamics, Quincy, Mass. WILLIAMS,LOPEZ and LUM-MUS were bought by MSC in Jan 2006 for £41million ($70 m) each. The remaining pair are owned and operated by American Overseas Marine.

1ST LT. HARRY L. MARTIN CLASS

Ship	Pennant Number	In Service	Builder
1st LT HARRY L. MARTIN	T-AK 3015	1979	Bremer Vulkan

Machinery One Bremer Vulkan MAN diesel driving one shaft; 25,700 shp **Displacement** 51,531 tonnes **Dimensions** 230m x 32.3m x 10.9m **Speed** 21.5 knots **Complement** 27 civilians, 12 military technicians.

Notes
USNS 1st LT. HARRY L. MARTIN was modified in 1999 and delivered to MSC in 2000. She is loaded with US Marine Corps equipment

MV Gunnery Sgt. Fred W. Stockham

GUNNERY SGT. FRED W. STOCKHAM CLASS

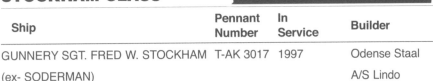

Ship	Pennant Number	In Service	Builder
GUNNERY SGT. FRED W. STOCKHAM	T-AK 3017	1997	Odense Staal
(ex- SODERMAN)			A/S Lindo

Machinery Two Burmeister & Wain diesels driving one shaft; 47,300shp **Displacement** 56,004 tonnes **Dimensions** 276.6m x 32.3m x 10.6m **Speed** 24 knots **Complement** 26

Notes

Built as commercial container ship in Denmark in 1980, the ship was acquired by the Navy in the early 1990s. Following conversion to her new role at NASSCo she was commissioned into Military Sealift Command in 1997 as USNS SODERMAN . In 2000, she transferred to the Maritime Prepositioning Force, and recommissioned in 2001, being re-named GYSGT FRED W. STOCKHAM.

LANCE CPL. ROY M. WHEAT CLASS

Ship	Pennant Number	In Service	Builder
LANCE CPL. ROY M. WHEAT	T-AK 3016	2003	Chernomorskiy Zavod, Ukraine

Machinery Two Mashproyect-Zorya M25 Gas Turbines driving two shafts; 18,000shp each **Displacement** 50,570 tons **Dimensions** 263.1m x 30.01m x 10.67m **Speed** 26.5 knots **Complement** 25

Notes

Pre-positions USMC equipment at sea, enabling rapid delivery during war or contingency.

One of more than 36 ships in MSC's Afloat Prepositioning Force that supports all U.S. military services. Assigned to Maritime Prepositioning Ship Squadron One in the Mediterranean.

Capt. Steven L. Bennett

CONTAINER SHIPS

CAPT. STEVEN L. BENNETT CLASS

Ship	Pennant Number	In Service	Builder
CAPT. STEVEN L. BENNETT	T-AK 4396	1984	Samsung, SK

Machinery 1 x Sulzer diesel driving one shaft; 16,320shp **Displacement** 54,589 tonnes **Dimensions** 209.4m x 30.4m x 11.6m **Speed** 11 knots **Complement** 26 civilians.

Notes
Carries US Air Force cargo and features a climate-controlled cocoon on the weather deck to allow the ship to carry approximately 50 percent more cargo, while protecting the additional cargo from the marine environment.

MV Maj. Bernard F. Fisher

LTC CALVIN P. TITUS

Ship	Pennant Number	In Service	Builder
MAJ. BERNARD F. FISHER	T-AK 4396	1985	Odense Staal A/S Lindo

Machinery 1 x Sulzer diesel driving one shaft; 23,030shp **Displacement** 48,000 tonnes **Dimensions** 198.86m x 32.24m x 10.99m **Speed** 19 knots **Complement** 21.

Notes

Owned and operated by Sealift Inc the ship is loaded with US Air Force cargo. The ship is self-sustaining, having cranes that allows it to off-load its own cargo.

MV A1C William A. Pitsenbarger

A1C WILLIAM A. PITSENBARGER CLASS

Ship	Pennant Number	In Service	Builder
A1C WILLIAM A. PITSENBARGER	T-AK 4638	1983	Ch. d'Atlantique

Machinery 1 x Sulzer diesel driving one shaft; 13,800shp **Displacement** 40,000 tonnes **Dimensions** 189.1m x 32.2m x 11.4m **Speed** 17.5 knots   **Complement** 23 civilians.

Notes

MV A1C WILLIAM A. PITSENBARGER is owned and operated by RR&VO, Ltd and carries US Air Force cargo. The ship features a climate-controlled coccoon on the weather decks that allows it to carry approximately 50 percent more cargo, while protecting the additional cargo from the marine environment.

MV TSgt John A. Chapman

BUFFALO SOLDIER CLASS

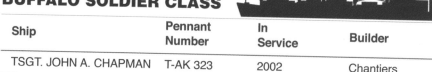

Ship	Pennant Number	In Service	Builder
TSGT. JOHN A. CHAPMAN	T-AK 323	2002	Chantiers

Machinery Pielstick medium speed diesel driving one shaft; 23,400shp **Displacement** 41,002 tonnes **Dimensions** 204.2m x 26.5m x 10.5m **Speed** 16 knots **Complement** 19

Notes

The former MV MERLIN, she was renamed in April 2005. Another vessel with an all-weather cocoon over the upperdeck, she is loaded with US Air Force munitions and other supplies. The ship is operated by Sealift Inc. of Oyster Bay, NY.

MVs Cornhusker State & Flickertail State

READY RESERVE FORCE

AUXILIARY CRANE SHIPS
KEYSTONE STATE CLASS

Ship	Pennant Number	To RRF	Builder
KEYSTONE STATE	T-ACS 1	1984	NASSCo
GEM STATE	T-ACS 2	1985	NASSCo
GRAND CANYON STATE	T-ACS 3	1987	NASSCo

Displacement 16,599 tonnes **Dimensions** 203.8m x 23.2m x 5.8m **Speed** 18 knots **Complement** 64

Notes
These ships are converted container ships with three twin boom pedestal cranes which can lift containers or other cargo from themselves or adjacent vessels and deposit the cargo on a pier or lighterage. Fitted with 3 twin 30 ton capacity cranes. The four forward cranes can be ganged together to lift 150 tons. Operated under contract by Pacific Gulf Marine.

GOPHER STATE CLASS

Ship	Pennant Number	To RRF	Builder
GOPHER STATE	T-ACS 4	1988	Bath Iron Works
FLICKERTAIL STATE	T-ACS 5	1988	Bath Iron Works
CORNHUSKER STATE	T-ACS 6	1988	Bath Iron Works

Displacement 26,670 tons **Dimensions** 205.7m x 24.4m x 10.3m **Speed** 18.9 knots **Complement** 52

Notes
Operated under contract by Interocean American Shipping Corporation.

DIAMOND STATE CLASS

Ship	Pennant Number	To RRF	Builder
DIAMOND STATE	T-ACS 7	1989	Todd SY, Ca
EQUALITY STATE	T-ACS 8	1989	Todd SY, Ca

Displacement 15,138 tonnes **Dimensions** 203.6m x 23.2m x 10.1m **Speed** 18.9 knots **Complement** 40

Notes

Fitted with 3 twin 30 ton cranes. Both transferred to the National Defence Reserve Force on 28 July 2006.

BEAVER STATE CLASS

Ship	Pennant Number	To RRF	Builder
GREEN MOUNTAIN STATE	T-ACS 9	1991	Ingalls SB
BEAVER STATE	T-ACS 10	1993	Ingalls SB

Displacement 11,720 tonnes **Dimensions** 198m x 23m x 10.1m **Speed** 21.6 knots **Complement** 64

Notes

Fitted with 3 twin 30 ton cranes mounted to starboard. Both transferred to the National Defence Reserve Force on 28 July 2006.

MV Cape Decision

ROLL ON/ROLL OFF SHIPS

ADMIRAL WM. M. CALLAGHAN CLASS

Ship	Pennant Number	In Service	Builder
ADM WM M. CALLAGHAN GTS	T-AKR 1001	1967	Sun SB & DD Co

Displacement 13,161 tonnes **Dimensions** 211.6m x 28m x 5.18m **Speed** 26 knots **Complement** 28

Notes

A ship of several 'firsts'. She was the first Ro-Ro built for the USN and initially operated under charter to MSC. She was also the first gas turbine powered vessel constructed for the USN. Originally powered by P&W FT-4s, these were replaced by the newer LM2500's in 1997. Has a capacity of 750 vehicles and 212 standard containers. Can offload using its own array of cranes (2 x 120 ton; 6 x 25 ton and 10 x 15 ton). Operated under contract by Patriot Contract Services, LLC. The ship is prefixed GTS for Gas Turbine Ship.

CAPE D CLASS

Ship	Pennant Number	To RRF	Builder
CAPE DECISION	T-AKR 5054	1985	Eriksberg
CAPE DIAMOND	T-AKR 5055	1985	Chantiers
CAPE DOMINGO	T-AKR 5053	1985	Chantiers
CAPE DOUGLAS	T-AKR 5052	1985	Eriksberg
CAPE DUCATO	T-AKR 5051	1985	Chantiers

Displacement 13,140 tons **Dimensions** 207.4m x 29.6m x 4.11m **Speed** 16 knots
Complement 27

Notes
Operated under contract by Marine Transport Lines.

CAPE E CLASS

Ship	Pennant Number	To RRF	Builder
CAPE EDMONT	T-AKR 5069	1987	Eriksberg

Displacement 12,256 tons **Dimensions** 199.1m x 28.7m x 3.8m **Speed** 16 knots
Complement 27

Notes
Operated under contract by Marine Transport Lines.

CAPE H CLASS

Ship	Pennant Number	To RRF	Builder
CAPE HENRY	T-AKR 5067	1986	Mitsubishi Heavy Ind
CAPE HORN	T-AKR 5068	1986	Kaldnes Mek Versted
CAPE HUDSON	T-AKR 5066	1986	Tangan Vaerft

Displacement 19,091 tons **Dimensions** 228.5m x 32.3m x 4.7m **Speed** 18 knots
Complement 28

Notes
All vary slightly in design. Each ship includes a 34,000 square foot hoistable deck. Four internal vehicle decks and can carry around 1600 standard 20ft containers. Operated under contract by Pacific Gulf Marine.

CAPE I CLASS

Ship	Pennant Number	To RRF	Builder
CAPE INSCRIPTION	T-AKR 5076	1987	Bath Iron Works
CAPE INTREPID	T-AKR 11	1986	Bath Iron Works
CAPE ISABEL	T-AKR 5062	1986	Bath Iron Works
CAPE ISLAND	T-AKR 10	1993	Bath Iron Works

Displacement 14,767 tons **Dimensions** 208.7m x 31m x 5.2m **Speed** 19.8 knots
Complement 31

Notes
Operated under contract by Crowley Liner Services Inc.

CAPE K CLASS

Ship	Pennant Number	To RRF	Builder
CAPE KENNEDY	T-AKR 5083	1995	Nippon Kokan
CAPE KNOX	T-AKR 5082	1995	Nippon Kokan

Displacement 36,450 tons Dimensions 212.1m x 32.3m x 10.72m Speed 17.6 knots Complement 25

Notes
Ships have two vehicle decks and can also be used to transport 1,550 standard 20ft containers. Operated under contract by Keystone Shipping Services Inc.

CAPE L CLASS

Ship	Pennant Number	To RRF	Builder
CAPE LAMBERT	T-AKR 5077	1987	Port Weller DD, Canada
CAPE LOBOS	T-AKR 5078	1987	Port Weller DD, Canada

Displacement 30,375 tons Dimensions 207.9m x 22.92m x 9.3m Speed 17.1 knots Complement 27

Notes
Former newsprint and vehicle carriers with ice strengthened hulls. Both transferred to the National Defence Reserve Force on 28 July 2006.

CAPE O CLASS

Ship	Pennant Number	To RRF	Builder
CAPE ORLANDO	T-AKR 2044	1994	Kokums AB Malmo

Displacement 12,500 tons Dimensions 193.63m x 28.01m x 3.94m Speed 17.1 knots Complement 25

Notes
Operated under contract by Patriot Contract Services LLC.

CAPE R CLASS

Ship	Pennant Number	To RRF	Builder
CAPE RACE	T-AKR 9960	1994	Kawasaki Heavy Ind
CAPE RAY	T-AKR 9679	1994	Kawasaki Heavy Ind
CAPE RISE	T-AKR 9678	1994	Kawasaki Heavy Ind

Displacement 32,000 tons **Dimensions** 197.52m x 32.26m x 8.5m **Speed** 17.6 knots
Complement 29 (Full Operating Status); 9 (Reserve)

Notes
Spar decks added in 1998 to provide additional vehicle capacity. Operated under contract by Keystone Shipping Services Inc.

CAPE T CLASS

Ship	Pennant Number	To RRF	Builder
CAPE TAYLOR	T-AKR 113	1994	Sasebo Heavy Ind
CAPE TEXAS	T-AKR 112	1994	HDW Kiel
CAPE TRINITY	T-AKR 9711	1994	HDW Kiel

Displacement 9,870 tons **Dimensions** 191.29m x 27.21m x 4.05m **Speed** 16.7 knots
Complement 27 (Full Operating Status); 9 (Reserve)

Notes
CAPE TAYLOR has a smaller cargo capacity. Operated under contract by Crowley Liner Services Inc.

CAPE V CLASS

Ship	Pennant Number	To RRF	Builder
CAPE VICTORY	T-AKR 9701	1993	Fincantieri
CAPE VINCENT	T-AKR 9666	1993	Fincantieri

Displacement 27,000 tons Dimensions 192m x 26.55m x 8.47m Speed 15 knots Complement 25

Notes
Spar decks added in 1998 to provide additional vehicle capacity. Operated under contract by Keystone Shipping Services Inc.

CAPE W CLASS

Ship	Pennant Number	To RRF	Builder
CAPE WASHINGTON	T-AKR 9961	1994	Stocznia, Poland
CAPE WRATH	T-AKR 9962	1994	Stocznia, Poland

Displacement 47,000 tons Dimensions 212.6m x 32.28m x 11.63m Speed 15.8 knots Complement 28

Notes
Former car carriers. Both have had their seven vehicle decks replaced by three stronger decks to accommodate military vehicles. Operated under contract by Crowley Liner Services Inc.

COMET CLASS

Ship	Pennant Number	To RRF	Builder
COMET	T-AKR 7	1985	Sun SB & DD Co

Displacement 7,605 tons Dimensions 152.1m x 23.77m x 4.29m Speed 16.2 knots Complement 44

Notes
Built in 1958, she had served with the Military Sealift Command until deactivated in 1984. She was transferred to MARAD in November 2001. Transferred to the National Defence Reserve Force on 28 July 2006.

METEOR CLASS

Ship	Pennant Number	To RRF	Builder
METEOR	T-AKR 9	1985	Puget Sound Bridge & DD

Displacement 9,154 tons Dimensions 164.7m x 25.5m x 4.5m Speed 18.9 knots Complement 44

Notes
Reclassified as a T-AKR in 1969. Since 2000 has been on 10 day recall at Suisun Bay, California. Was transferred to MARAD in 2001. Transferred to the National Defence Reserve Force on 28 July 2006.

Cape Fear

LIGHTER ABOARD SHIPS

Ship	Pennant Number	To RRF	Builder
CAPE FAREWELL	T-AKR 5073	1987	Avondale SY
CAPE FLATTERY	T-AKR 5070	1987	Avondale SY

Displacement 16,490 tons **Dimensions** 272.3m x 30.56m x 4.42m **Speed** 19.8 knots **Complement** 31

Notes
Has 455 ton travelling crane to handle 89 LASH Lighters (barges) which carry pre-loaded cargo. They are floated on and off at the stern.

Ship	Pennant Number	To RRF	Builder
CAPE FEAR	T-AKR 5061	1985	Avondale SY
CAPE FLORIDA	T-AKR 5071	1987	Avondale SY

Displacement 14,230 tons **Dimensions** 249.9m x 30.5m x 4.6m **Speed** 19.8 knots **Complement** 31

Notes
Has 30 ton travelling crane to handle 77 LASH Lighters. Also equipped with two 5 ton cranes. All four ships are operated under contract by Patriot Contract Services LLC. CAPE FLORIDA and CAPE FEAR were transferred to the National Defence Reserve Force on 28 July 2006.

Cape Girardeau

BREAKBULK SHIPS

Ship	Pennant Number	To RRF	Builder
CAPE GIBSON	T-AK 5051	1988	Newport News SB & DD
CAPE GIRARDEAU	T-AK 2039	1988	Newport News SB & DD
CAPE JACOB	T-AK 5029	1986	Newport News SB & DD

Displacement 9,790 tons (8,280 JACOB) **Dimensions** 184.4m x 25.1m x 9.5m (161.1m x 23.2m x 4.7m JACOB) **Speed** 17.9 knots (17 knots JACOB) **Complement** 32-38

Notes
The term "breakbulk ships" refers to ships characterised by large open hatches and fitted with boom and winch gear or deck cranes. Commercially overtaken by containerships, they are however ideally suited for military sealift. They can be used at ports that lack their own off loading facilities . All three ships are fitted with the Modular Cargo Delivery System (MCDS) which allows them to perform standard tensioned alongside replenishment operations with US and Allied ships equipped with a dry cargo receiving station. The MCDS is a self-contained station installed on the port side forward and aft. In addition all ships are fitted with a flightdeck to allow vertical replenishment operations. CAPE JACOB is operated under contract by Matson Navigation Company. CAPE GIBSON and CAPE GIRADEAU are operated by Patriot Contract Services LLC. CAPE JACOB has been activated for duty with the Prepositioning Programme.

124

MV Cape Mohican

SEABEE SHIP

Ship	Pennant Number	To RRF	Builder
CAPE MAY	T-AKR 5063	1986	GD Quincy
CAPE MOHICAN	T-AKR 5065	1986	GD Quincy

Displacement 18,880 tons **Dimensions** 266.4m x 32.3m x 5.4m **Speed** 17.1 knots
Complement 34

Notes

The SEABEE is arranged much differently from the LASH configured vessels in that it has three decks on which the cargo barges or container flats are stowed. Barges are brought to each deck level by a stern elevator and are moved internally within the ship by the Transporter (conveyor) System. Two barges can be loaded or discharged in about 40 minutes. These ships have a capacity of 38 barges. Operated under Contract by Ocean Duchess Inc.

USN & USMC AVIATION

US Naval aviation is one of the world's most powerful air forces, operating around 3,800 aircraft. Operating 12 aircraft carriers and 11 'flat-top' Amphibious vessels, the aircraft of the USN and USMC are able to project power from the sea, deep inland, with the USMC traditionally concentrating on providing troops ashore with close air support and amphibious airlift.

The USN operate ten Carrier Air Wings (CVW) each comprising fixed wing aircraft squadrons capable of undertaking most warfare roles, fighter; strike; electronic warfare; airborne early warning; sea control and aerial refuelling. In addition two helicopter squadrons are also operated. There is usually a fixed wing logistic detachment of two aircraft embarked for cargo, mail and personnel transfer between ship and shore.

A typical CVW is likely to include four squadrons of F/A-18 Hornet (48 aircraft); four EA-6B Prowlers; four E-2C Hawkeye; eight S-3B Viking and two C-2A Greyhound aircraft. The two helicopter squadrons (20 aircraft) are spread throughout ships of the Carrier Strike Group.

The USN also maintains a significant force of land-based aircraft for both frontline and support roles. The traditional submarine hunting and maritime surveillance roles of the P-3 Orion has been augmented in recent years giving the aircraft a potent strike capability.

An important part of US Naval aviation remains the Naval Air Force Reserve, providing aircraft and crews to augment the fleet. As with many other facets of naval aviation, the Naval Air Force Reserve is also undergoing a drastic reorganisation. A new concept - the Active-Reserve Integration plan will see much of the Reserve infrastructure removed, as well as the squadrons, as the aircraft and aircrew become more aligned with the active component of naval aviation. However, some reserve squadrons will remain, particularly those specialist squadrons performing such roles as airlift support and flight adversary roles.

US Naval aviation is going through quite a transition in terms of both aircraft and organisation. The venerable F-14 Tomcat has now paid off from service, to be replaced by the F/A-18 Super Hornet. The S-3B is coming to the end of its service life, the ASW role having been taken over by the MH-60 helicopter and its tanking role eventually being adopted by the F/A-18. Another aircraft in the twilight of its career is the EA-6B Prowler. This elderly electronic warfare aircraft will be replaced in service by another version of the ubiquitous F/A-18 Super Hornet - the EA-18 Growler, which in 2006 began test flying with Boeing. The helicopter community is being re-organised and (in 2007) is in the middle of a major transition in role and aircraft type (see page 140).

Since 2002 the USN and USMC have been slowly implementing the Tactical Avaition

Integration Plan, whereby strike fighter and EW squadrons from both services are being pooled to provide flexibility, with a USMC squadron being assigned to each CVW, alhough commitments in Iraq have somewhat stalled this plan. The integration plan also committed the USN to deactivating three Hornet squadrons and dedicated three further squadrons to rotation in Japan under the USMC deployment programme.

On the horizon is the introdution into service of the F-35 Joint Strike Fighter for both the USN and USMC in around 2013, while the USMC have recently seen the introduction into service of the MV-22 Osprey tilt-rotor aircraft.

US Naval Air Power in action! The aircraft carriers USS RONALD REAGAN (CVN 76), USS KITTY HAWK (CV 63) and USS ABRAHAM LINCOLN (CVN 72) sail in close formation at the start of Exercise Valiant Shield 2006. • US NAVY/CPH SPIKE CALL

AIRCRAFT OF THE UNITED STATES NAVY
Squadron Numbers

Squadron	Nickname	Squadron	Nickname
FA-18 Super Hornet		VFA-136	KNIGHTHAWKS
		VFA-137	KESTRELS
VFA-2	BOUNTY HUNTERS	VFA-146	BLUE DIAMONDS
VFA-11	RED RIPPERS	VFA-147	ARGONAUTS
VFA-14	TOPHATTERS	VFA-151	FIGHTING VIGILANTES
VFA-22	FIGHTING REDCOCKS	VFA-192	GOLDEN DRAGONS
VFA-31	TOMCATTERS	VFA-195	DAMBUSTERS
VFA-32	SWORDSMEN	VFA-201(R)	HUNTERS
VFA-41	BLACK ACES	VFA-204(R)	RIVER RATTLERS
VFA-102	DIAMONDBACKS	VFC-12(R)	FIGHTING OMARS
VFA-103	JOLLY ROGERS		
VFA-115	EAGLES	**EA-6B Prowler**	
VFA-143	PUKING DOGS		
VFA-154	BLACK KNIGHTS	VAQ-129	VIKINGS
VFA-211	FLYING CHECKMATES	VAQ-130	ZAPPERS
VFA-213	BLACK LIONS	VAQ-131	LANCERS
		VAQ-132	SCORPIONS
FA-18 Hornet		VAQ-133	WIZARDS
		VAQ-134	GARUDAS
VFA-15	VALIONS	VAQ-135	BLACK RAVENS
VFA-25	FIST OF THE FLEET	VAQ-136	GAUNTLETS
VFA-27	CHARGERS	VAQ-137	ROOKS
VFA-34	BLUE BLASTERS	VAQ-138	YELLOWJACKETS
VFA-37	BULLS	VAQ-139	COUGARS
VFA-81	SUNLINERS	VAQ-140	PATRIOTS
VFA-83	RAMPAGERS	VAQ-141	SHADOWHAWKS
VFA-86	SIDEWINDERS	VAQ-142	GRAY WOLVES
VFA-87	GOLDEN WARRIORS	VAQ-209(R)	STAR WARRIORS
VFA-94	MIGHTY SHRIKES		
VFA-97	WARHAWKS	**S-3 Viking**	
VFA-105	GUNSLINGERS		
VFA-106	GLADIATORS	VS-22	CHECKMATES
VFA-113	STINGERS	VS-24	SCOUTS
VFA-122	FLYING EAGLES	VS-31	TOP CATS
VFA-125	ROUGH RAIDERS	VS-32	MAULERS
VFA-131	WILDCATS		

Squadron	Nickname	Squadron	Nickname
E-2C Hawkeye		VP-47	GOLDEN SWORDSMEN
		VP-62(R)	BROAD ARROWS
VAW-77(R)	NIGHT WOLVES	VP-69(R)	TOTEMS
VAW-112	GOLDEN HAWKS	VP-92(R)	MINUTEMEN
VAW-113	BLACK EAGLES	VQ-1	WORLD WATCHERS
VAW-115	LIBERTY BELLS	VQ-2	BATMEN
VAW-116	SUN KINGS	VPU-1	OLD BUZZARDS
VAW-117	WALLBANGERS	VPU-2	WIZARDS
VAW-120	GREYHAWKS		
VAW-121	BLUETAILS	**C-130 Hercules**	
VAW-123	SCREWTOPS		
VAW-124	BEAR ACES	VR-53 (R)	CAPITAL EXPRESS
VAW-125	TIGERTAILS	VR-54 (R)	REVELERS
VAW-126	SEAHAWKS	VR-55 (R)	MINUTEMEN
		VR-62 (R)	NOR'EASTERS
C-2A Greyhound		VR-64 (R)	THE CONDORS
VRC-30	PROVIDERS	**C-9B Skytrain**	
VRC-40	RAWHIDES		
		VR-46(R)	EAGLES
E-6B Mercury		VR-52(R)	THE TASKMASTERS
		VR-56(R)	GLOBEMASTERS
VQ-3	IRONMEN	VR-61(R)	ISLANDERS
VQ-4	SHADOWS		
VQ-7	ROUGHNECKS	**C-40A Clipper**	
P-3/EP-3 Orion		VR-57	CONQUISTADORES
		VR-58	SUNSEEKERS
VP-1	SCREAMING EAGLES	VR-59	LONE STAR EXPRESS
VP-4	SKINNY DRAGONS		
VP-5	MAD FOXES	**C-20G Gulfstream**	
VP-8	TIGERS		
VP-9	GOLDEN EAGLES	VR-48	CAPITAL SKYLINERS
VP-10	RED LANCERS	VR-51	WINDJAMMERS
VP-16	WAR EAGLES		
VP-26	TRIDENTS	**T-6A Texan II**	
VP-30	PRO'S NEST		
VP-40	FIGHTING MARLINS	VT-4	WARBUCKS
VP-45	PELICANS	VT-10	WILDCATS
VP-46	GREY KNIGHTS		

Squadron	Nickname	Squadron	Nickname

T-39 Sabreliner

VT-86	SABRE HAWKS

T-34C Turbo Mentor

VT-2	DOER BIRDS
VT-3	RED KNIGHTS
VT-6	SHOOTERS
VT-27	BOOMERS
VT-28	RANGERS

T-45 Goshawk

VT-7	EAGLES
VT-9	TIGERS
VT-21	REDHAWKS
VT-22	GOLDEN EAGLES

T-2 Buckeye

VT-86	SABRE HAWKS

T-44 Pegasus

VT-31	WISE OWLS
VT-35	STINGRAYS

SH/MH-60 Seahawk

The Seahawk squadrons began a major shift in role and deployment with the introduction of the MH-60S and MH-60R. HS and HC squadrons are being redesignated HSC (Helicopter Sea Combat). HSL squadrons are being redesignated HSM (Helicopter Maritime Strike). In many cases the prefix change also results in a number change (eg HC-5 PROVIDERS became HSC-25 ISLAND KNIGHTS).

The following list of squadrons therefore is likely to change significantly over the coming years as the multi role MH-60S/R aircraft replace the SH-60B/F in more significant numbers.

HS-2	GOLDEN FALCONS
HS-3	TRIDENTS
HS-4	BLACK KNIGHTS
HS-5	NIGHTDIPPERS
HS-6	INDIANS
HS-7	DUSTY DOGS
HS-8	EIGHT-BALLERS
HS-10	WAR HAWKS
HS-11	DRAGONSLAYERS
HS-14	CHARGERS
HS-15	RED LIONS
HS-75 (R)	EMERALD KNIGHTS
HSC-2	FLEET ANGELS
HSC-3	MERLINS
HSC-4 (R)	RED WOLVES
HSC-5 (R)	FIREHAWKS
HSC-21	BLACKJACKS
HSC-22	SEA KNIGHTS
HSC-23	WILDCARDS
HSC-25	ISLAND KNIGHTS
HSC-26	CHARGERS
HSC-28	BAY RAIDERS
HSC-85	GOLDEN GATORS
HSL-37	EASY RIDERS
HSL-40	AIRWOLVES
HSL-42	PROUD WARRIORS
HSL-43	BATTLE CATS
HSL-44	SWAMP FOX
HSL-45	WOLFPACK
HSL-46	GRANDMASTERS
HSL-47	SABERHAWKS
HSL-48	VIPERS
HSL-49	SCORPIONS
HSL-51	WARLORDS
HSL-60(R)	JAGUARS

Squadron	Nickname	Squadron	Nickname
HSM-41	SEAHAWKS	HM-15(R)	BLACKHAWKS
TH-57 Sea Ranger		**Operational Test & Evaluation**	
HT-8	EIGHTBALLERS	VX-1	PIONEERS
HT-18	VIGILANT EAGLES	VX-9	VAMPIRES
		VX-20	FORCE
MH-53E Sea Dragon		VX-21	ROTARY TEST
		VX-23	SALTY DOGS
HC-4	BLACK STALLIONS	VX-31	DUST DEVILS
HM-14(R)	VANGUARD	VXS-1	WARLOCKS

AIRCRAFT OF THE US MARINE CORPS
Squadron Numbers

Marine Corps aviation is organised differently to the USN. There are four Marine Air Wings (MAW) and within each MAW there are three to four Marine Air Groups (MAG). Each MAG can be assigned any number of squadrons, each with differing roles and aircraft. In some cases aircraft can be drawn from individual squadrons and assigned to a composite squadron - so for example it is not unusual to see fixed wing Harrier aircraft assigned to a Heavy Lift Helicopter squadron. To make this section easier to read, where more than one type of aircraft is commonly assigned to a squadron, I have listed those squadrons by role, rather than aircraft type.

Squadron	Nickname	Squadron	Nickname
FA-18 Hornet (All Weather)		VMFA-122	CRUSADERS
		VMFA-134	SMOKES
VMFA(AW)-121	GREEN KNIGHTS	VMFA-142	FLYING GATORS
VMFA(AW)-224	BENGALS	VMFA-212	LANCERS
VMFA(AW)-225	THE VIKINGS	VMFA-232	RED DEVILS
VMFA(AW)-242	BATS	VMFA-251	THUNDERBOLTS
VMFA(AW)-332	MOONLIGHTERS	VMFA-312	CHECKERBOARDS
VMFA(AW)-533	HAWKS	VMFA-314	BLACK KNIGHTS
		VMFA-321	HELLS ANGELS
FA-18 Hornet		VMFA-323	DEATH RATTLERS
		VMFA-533	KNIGHTHAWKS
VMFA-112	COWBOYS	VMFAT-101	SHARPSHOOTERS
VMFA-115	SILVER EAGLES		

Squadron	Nickname	Squadron	Nickname
AV-8 Harrier		HMH-362	UGLY ANGELS
		HMH-363	RED LIONS
VMA-211	AVENGERS	HMH-461	IRON HORSES
VMA-214	BLACKSHEEP	HMH-462	HEAVY HAULERS
VMA-223	BULLDOGS	HMH-463	HEAVY HAULERS
VMA-231	ACE OF SPADES	HMH-464	CONDORS
VMA-311	GREYHAWKS	HMH-465	WAR HORSES
VMA-513	NIGHTMARE	HMH-466	WOLFPACK
VMA-542	TIGERS	HMH-769	ROAD HOGS
VMAT-203	HAWKS	HMH-772	HUSLTERS
EA-6B Prowler		**Medium Helicopter**	
VMAQ-1	BANSHEES	HMM-161	GREY HAWKS
VMAQ-2	PLAYBOYS	HMM-163	EVIL EYES
VMAQ-3	MOONDOGS	HMM-165	WHITE KNIGHTS
VMAQ-4	SEAHAWKS	HMM-166	SEA ELKS
		HMM-261	RAGING BULLS
Tanker and Transport		HMM-262	FLYING TIGERS
		HMM-264	BLACK KNIGHTS
VMGR-152	SUMOS	HMM-265	DRAGONS
VMGR-234	THUNDER HERD	HMM-268	RED DRAGONS
VMGR-252	HEAVY HAULERS	HMM-364	PURPLE FOXES
VMGR-352	THE RAIDERS	HMM-365	BLUE KNIGHTS
VMGR-452	YANKEES	HMM-764	MOONLIGHT
		HMM-774	HONKERS
Dissimilar Air Combat		HMMT-164	FLYING CLAYMORES
VMFT-401	SNIPERS	**Light/Attack Helicopter**	
V-22 Osprey		HMLA-167	WARRIORS
		HMLA-169	VIPERS
VMM-162	GOLDEN EAGLES	HMLA-267	BLACK ACES
VMM-263	THUNDER CHICKENS	HMLA-269	SEA COBRAS
VMM-266	FIGHTING GRIFFINS	HMLA-367	SCARFACES
VMMT-204	RAPTORS	HMLA-369	GUNFIGHTERS
		HMLA-773	COBRAS
Heavy Helicopter		HMLA-775	COYOTES
		HMT-302	PHOENIX
HMH-361	FLYING TIGERS	HMT-303	ATLAS

Boeing F/A-18 SUPER HORNET

Variants F/A-18E; F/A-18F
Role Multi-role attack and fighter aircraft
Engines Two F414-GE-400 turbofan engines. 22,000 pounds (9,977 kg) static thrust per engine.
Length 18.5 metres **Height** 4.87 metres **Wingspan** 13.68 metres
Weight Maximum Take Off Gross Weight 29,932 kg
Speed Mach 1.8+ **Ceiling** 50,000+ feet
Range Combat - 1,275 nautical miles, clean plus two AIM-9s; Ferry - 1,660 nautical miles, two AIM-9s, three 480 gallon tanks retained.
Crew E model: One; F model: Two.
Armament One M61A1/A2 Vulcan 20mm cannon; AIM 9 Sidewinder, AIM-9X (projected), AIM 7 Sparrow, AIM-120 AMRAAM, Harpoon, Harm, SLAM, SLAM-ER (projected), Maverick missiles; Joint Stand-Off Weapon (JSOW); Joint Direct Attack Munition (JDAM); Data Link Pod; Paveway Laser Guided Bomb; various general purpose bombs, mines and rockets

Notes
The F/A-18E/F provides the carrier strike group with a strike fighter that has significant growth potential and increased range, endurance and ordnance-carrying capabilities over its predecessors. The F/A-18E/F has replaced the F-14 and early model F/A-18s.. Pacific Fleet aircraft are based at NAS Lemoore, California. The first Super Hornet squadron was forward deployed to NAF Atsugi, Japan in November 2003. NAS Oceana, Virginia and MCAS Cherry Point, North Carolina are the Atlantic Fleet home bases. 432 aircraft are on order, to be delivered by 2009.

Boeing F/A-18 HORNET

Variants F/A-18A; F/A-18B; F/A-18C; F/A-18D
Role All-weather attack and fighter aircraft
Engines Two F404-GE-400 turbofan engines. 16,000 pounds static thrust each.
Length 17.06 metres **Height** 4.87 metres **Wingspan** 11.43 metres
Speed Mach 1.8+. **Ceiling** 50,000+ feet
Range Fighter mission - 400 nautical miles; Attack mission - 575 nautical miles; Ferry - 2,000 nautical miles.
Crew A/C model: One; B/D model: Two.
Armament One M61A1/A2 Vulcan 20mm cannon; AIM 9 Sidewinder, AIM-9X (projected), AIM 7 Sparrow, AIM-120 AMRAAM, Harpoon, Harm, SLAM, SLAM-ER (projected), Maverick missiles; Joint Stand-Off Weapon (JSOW); Joint Direct Attack Munition (JDAM); Data Link Pod; Paveway Laser Guided Bomb; various general purpose bombs, mines and rockets

Notes

The F/A-18 Hornet is Naval Aviation's principal strike-fighter. This state-of-the-art, multi-mission aircraft serves in both the USN and Marine Corps. Although the F/A-18A to D are out of production, the existing inventory of approximately 681 Navy and Marine Corps aircraft will continue to comprise half of Naval Aviation's strike assets through 2012, and will continue to serve in active squadrons until 2023.

There are 30 Active USN squadrons and three reserve. The United States Marines Corps (USMC) operate 168 aircraft in 10 active and four reserve squadrons.

Grumman F-14 TOMCAT

Variants F-14B; F-14D
Role Fleet Air Defence, Recce and Ground Attack
Propulsion F-14B/D: (2) F110-GE400 Afterburning Turbofans with over 54,000 lb Total Thrust.
Length 18.9 metres **Height** 4.8 metres
Wingspan 19 metres unswept; 11.4 metres swept.
Weight 43,600 lb (19,777 kg) (F-14B)
Airspeed Mach 2+ **Ceiling** 50,000+ feet **Range** 1600 nautical miles
Armament 20mm MK-61 Vulcan cannon; Sparrow, Sidewinder and Phoenix air-toair missiles; laser-guided and general purpose bombs
Crew Two (pilot and radar intercept officer)

Notes

2006 saw the final chapter in the career of this aircraft, which, thanks largely to the movie *Top Gun* defined naval aviation for a generation. The F-14 was a supersonic, twin-engine, variable sweep-wing fighter designed to attack and destroy enemy aircraft by day and night and in all weather conditions. The F-14 could track up to 24 targets simultaneously with its advanced weapons control system and engage any of them at long range with one of its six Phoenix missiles while continuing to scan the airspace. The final two squadrons, VF-213 Black Lions and VF-31 Tomcatters returned to NAS Oceana in March 2006 having completed a combat tour in the Gulf aboard USS THEODORE ROOSEVELT. They were officially retired in September 2006 and have been replaced in service by the F/A-18 Super Hornet.

Lockheed S-3 VIKING

Variants S-3B
Role Force Protection, Organic overhead/mission tanking.
Engines Two General Electric TF-34-GE-400B turbofan engines (9,275 pounds of thrust each)
Length 16 metres **Height** 6.9 metres **Wingspan** 20.6 metres
Weight Max design gross take-off: 52,539 pounds (23,643 kg)
Airspeed 450 knots **Ceiling** 40,000 feet
Range 2,300+ nautical miles
Crew One pilot; two flight officers and one sensor operator
Armament Up to 3,958 pounds (1,781 kg) of AGM-84 Harpoon, AGM-65 Maverick and AGM-84 SLAM missiles, torpedoes, rockets and bombs

Notes

Primarily designed for anti-submarine and anti-surface warfare, it has proved extremely versatile in service and can be equipped for in flight refuelling, sea control and limited electronic surveillance. The S-3B Viking community was selected for retirement in October 2002, which will be coordinated with the service entry of the F/A-18E/F Super Hornet tanker-capable aircraft through 2009. All avionics/navigation/computer upgrade programmes required to safely sustain the aircraft through its projected retirement schedule have been completed.

Grumman E-2 HAWKEYE

Variants E-2C
Role Airborne Command & Control, Battle Space Management
Engines Two Allison T-56-A427 turboprop engines; (5,100 shaft horsepower each)
Length 17.5 metres **Height** 5.6 metres **Wingspan** 28 metres
Weight Max. gross, take-off: 53,000 lbs (23,850 kg) 40,200 lbs basic (18,090 kg)
Airspeed 300+ knots
Ceiling 30,000 feet
Crew Five (two pilots, three mission systems operators)

Notes

Usually the first aircraft to launch and the last to recover from any carrier launched mission, it provides airborne early warning and command and control functions for a battle group. Additional missions include: surface surveillance co-ordination, strike and interceptor control, search and rescue guidance and communications relay. The ten fleet squadrons fly E-2C Group II and Hawkeye 2000 variants of the aircraft. An E-2D Advanced Hawkeye is under development by Northrop Grumman. Flight testing began in 2007 with a scheduled in service date of 2011. The new aircraft will feature a non-rotating ALD-18 AESA radar, though it will still be housed in the circular radome.

Grumman EA-6 PROWLER

Variants EA-6B
Role Electronic countermeasures
Propulsion Two Pratt & Whitney J52-P408 engines (10,400 pounds thrust each).
Length 17.7 metres **Height** 4.9 metres **Wingspan** 15.9 metres
Weight Maximum Take Off Gross Weight 61,500 pounds (27,450 kg).
Airspeed 500 kts + **Ceiling** 37,600 feet
Armament ALQ-99 Tactical Jamming System; HARM missiles
Range 1,000 nautical miles+
Crew Pilot and three electronic countermeasures officers

Notes

The ALQ-00 TJS is used to provide active radar jamming support to attack aircraft, as well as ground units. Additional suppression of enemy air defences (SEAD) can be achieved through the HARM missile system.   An Improved Capability (ICAP) III upgrade achieved operational capability in September 2005. This generational leap in electronic attack capability deployed for the first time in 2006. The ICAP III includes a completely redesigned receiver system (ALQ-218), new displays, and MIDS/Link-16, which will dramatically improve joint interoperability. Additionally, the ALQ-218 will also form the heart of the EA-18G Growler – the follow on platform for the EA-6B based on the Super Hornet. The EA-18G is on schedule and under budget as it progresses toward its 2009 Initial Operating Capability. The aircraft completed its Critical Design Review (CDR) in April 2005 and flew its first flight towards the end of 2006. It is planned to acquire 90 aircraft to support a 10-squadron force. Initial procurement of the first four aircraft began in 2006. In addition to USN squadrons, four squadrons of EA-6B Prowlers are operated by the USMC, primarily from land bases.

Boeing AV-8B HARRIER

Variants AV-8B; AV-8B II+; TAV-8B
Role Day/Night ground attack
Engine One Rolls Royce F402-RR-408 turbofan engine
Thrust 23,400 pounds
Length 14.11 metres **Wing span** 9.24 metres
Armament Mk-82 series 500lbs bombs, Mk-83 series 1000lbs bombs, GBU-12 500lbs laser guided bombs, GBU-16 1000lbs laser guided bombs, AGM-65F IR Maverick missiles, AGM-65E Laser Maverick missiles, CBU-99 cluster munitions, AIM-9M sidewinders, Lightening II targeting POD to deliver GBU-12 and GBU-16 bombs with pinpoint accuracy.
Crew 1

Notes

Operated by the USMC from large amphibious flat tops or shore bases, this Vertical Take-off and Landing aircraft is developed from the original UK Harrier. The prime mission of the aircraft is close air support for ground troops. Two variants of the aircraft are in service operationally: the Night Attack and the Radar/Night Attack Harrier. The Night Attack Harrier improved upon the original AV-8B design through the incorporation of a Navigation, Forward-Looking InfraRed (NAVFLIR) sensor, a moving map, night vision goggle compatibility, and a higher performance engine. The current Radar/Night Attack Harrier, or Harrier II+, has all the improvements of the Night Attack aircraft plus the AN/APG-65 multi-mode radar. The two-seat TAV-8B trainers are undergoing an upgrade that adds new colour displays, night vision goggle-compatible lighting, and a more powerful and reliable Rolls Royce Pegasus (408) engine. The USMC operate 7 squadrons with 16 aircraft each and 1 training squadron.

HELICOPTER TRANSITION PLAN

Since 2002 the USN has been undergoing a major re-organisation and transition of current helicopter squadrons to the MH-60R/S Seahawk. It will take twelve years to complete the transition and the three traditional helicopter communities (HS - Anti-Submarine; HSL - Helicopter Anti-Submarine Light and HC - Helicopter Combat Support) will be reduced to two communities with an additional six squadrons.

The aim is to convert to a single aircraft type (MH-60R/S) with the Seirra variant assuming the logistics and SAR role and the Romeo variant taking over the anti-submarine and surface strike roles. Ten HS squadrons and five HC squadrons will be redesignated HSC (Helicopter Sea Combat). The reorganisation will include the commissioning of two extra HSC squadrons. Ten HSL squadrons will be redesignated HSM (Helicopter Maritime Strike) and re-equipped with the Romeo. An additional five HSM squadrons will be commissioned.

Deployment of the aircraft will also change significantly with each Carrier Air Wing being equipped with two squadrons, one of each type. These aircraft can then be redeployed to other ships within the Carrier Strike Group (CSG), but still be administered from, and under the command of, the CSG. The new structure will see four MH-60Rs remain on the carrier, with eight being based on ships within the group. The MH-60S squadron of eight aircraft will see two being deployed to the group's logistics ship.

A further six HSC squadrons would be available for deployment from Amphibious Assault ships. It is anticipated that the HSC squadrons will also adopt the airborne MCM role.

SQUADRON TRANSITION SCHEDULE

Old	New	Date	Old	New	Date
HS-2	HSC-12	Apr 2009	HSL-42	HSM-42	Mar 2014
HS-3	HSC-9	Feb 2010	New Squadron	HSM-70	Jan 2008
HS-4	HSC-4	Feb 2007	New Squadron	HSM-71	Apr 2009
HS-5	HSC-5	Feb 2009	New Squadron	HSM-72	Feb 2009
HS-6	HSC-6	Apr 2010	HSL-43	HSM-73	Feb 2007
HS-7	HSC-7	Jan 2008	HSL-44	HSM-74	Feb 2010
HS-8	HSC-8	Mar 2008	HSL-45	HSM-75	Mar 2008
HS-11	HSC-11	Feb 2011	HSL-46	HSM-76	Feb 2011
HS-14	HSC-14	Apr 2011	HSL-47	HSM-77	Apr 2010
HS-15	HSC-15	Feb 2012	New Squadron	HSM-78	Feb 2012
New Squadron	HSC-22	Jan 2007	New Squadron	HSM-79	Apr 2011
New Squadron	HSC-23	Jan 2007	HSL-48	HSM-48	Feb 2015
HSL-37	HSM-37	Jan 2014	HSL-49	HSM-49	Apr 2014
HSL-40	HSM-40	Jan 2010	HSL-51	HSM-51	Mar 2013
HSL-41	HSM-41	Mar 2005			

Sikorsky SH-60/MH-60 SEAHAWK

Variants SH-60B; SH-60F; MH-60S; MH-60R; VH-60N
Role ASW; Anti-shipping strike; SAR; Cargo Lift
Engines Two General Electric T700-GE-700 or T700-GE-701C engines
Length 19.6 metres **Height** 3.9 to 5.1 metres **Rotor Diameter** 16.4 metres
Weight 21,000 to 23,000 pounds (9,450 to 10,350 kg)
Airspeed 180 knots maximum
Range Approx 380 nautical miles **Crew** 3 - 4

Notes
The MH-60R and MH-60S multi-mission combat helicopters deploy as companion squadrons embarked in the Navy's aircraft carriers, surface warships, and logistics ships. The MH-60R provides surface and undersea warfare support with a suite of sensors and weapons that include low frequency (dipping) sonar, electronic support measures, advanced Forward Looking Infrared, and precision air-to-surface missiles. The MH-60S provides mine warfare support and will partner the MH-60R for surface warfare missions carrying the same Forward Looking Infrared air-to-ground sensors and weapons. The MH-60S can be reconfigured to provide Combat Search and Rescue and Naval Special Warfare support in joint operations. Airborne mine countermeasures operations will be accomplished using advanced sensor and weapon packages to provide detection, localisation, and neutralisation to anti-access threats. The MH-60S will conduct the fleet logistics role in carrier strike group and expeditionary strike group operations. MH-60R/S helicopters are produced with 85 percent common components (e.g., common cockpit and dynamic components) to simplify maintenance, logistics, and training. The MH-60R completed its Operational Evaluation in 2005 and is scheduled for a full-rate production decision in 2006. The Navy plans to acquire 254 MH-60Rs. The MH-60S was approved for full-rate production in August 2002 and is undergoing scheduled block upgrades for combat and airborne mine counter-measure missions. The Navy plans to acquire 271 MH-60S aircraft. In time these will replace the older SH-60B and SH-60F helicopters.   The VH-60N is flown by Marine Helicopter Squadron One (HMX-1) and supports the executive transport mission for the President of the United States.

US NAVY/PH3 CHRIS OTSEN

Sikorsky H-3 SEA KING

Variants SH-3H; UH-3H; VH-3D
Role Executive Transport; Utility and Torpedo recovery; Logistics/Search & Rescue
Engines Two General Electric T58-GE-402 turboshaft engines
Length 21.9 metres **Fuselage length** 16.5 metres **Height** 5.1 metres
Weight 11,865 lbs. (5,339 kg) empty; Maximum takeoff weight is 21,000 pounds (9,450 kg)
Airspeed 120 kts **Ceiling** 14,700 feet **Range** 542 nautical miles
Crew Four

Notes

First deployed in 1961 this work horse of the fleet is coming to the end of its service life and now remains in small numbers operating in various second line roles.

The VH-3D/VH-60N presidential helicopter replacement, recently designated VH-71A, is a conventional helicopter based on the Agusta Westland EH-101. It will provide safe and timely transportation for the President and Vice President of the United States, foreign heads of state, and others as directed by the White House Military Office. When the President is onboard Marine One, this aircraft is the Commander-in-Chief's primary command and control platform and must provide him with the flexibility and capabilities necessary to execute the duties of his office. Its capabilities, which will be delivered in two increments, are split into four functional areas: aircraft operations, communications, survivability, and Presidential accommodation. The VH-71A will have increased capabilities in these areas, while retaining core capabilities carried forward from the VH-3D and VH-60N variants.

Boeing CH-46 SEA KNIGHT

Variants CH-46E
Role Medium lift assault helicopter
Engines Two GE-T58-16 engines
Length Rotors unfolded: 25.69 metres Rotors folded 13.89 metres
Width Rotors unfolded: 15.54 metres Rotors folded4.49 metres
Height 5.08 metres
Maximum takeoff weight 24,300 pounds (11,032 kilograms)
Range 132 nautical miles for an assault mission
Speed 145 knots **Ceiling** 10,000 feet +
Crew Normal: 4 - pilot, co-pilot, crew chief, and 1st mechanic Combat: 5 - pilot, co-pilot, crew chief, and 2 aerial gunners
Payload Combat: maximum of 14 troops with aerial gunners; Medical evacuation: 15 litters and 2 attendants; Cargo: maximum of 4,000 pound (2,270 kilograms) external load

Notes

In a Marine Medium Helicopter (HMM) squadron the Sea Knight provides all-weather, day/night, night vision goggle (NVG) assault transport of combat troops, supplies, and equipment during amphibious and subsequent operations ashore. Troop assault is the primary function and the movement of supplies and equipment is secondary. Additional tasks comprise combat and assault support for evacuation operations and other maritime special operations; over-water search and rescue support; support for mobile forward refueling and rearming points and aeromedical evacuation of casualties from the field to suitable medical facilities.

Sikorsky CH-53 SEA STALLION

Variants RH-53D; CH-53E
Role Air Assault; Heavy transport
Engines Three GE T64-GE-416 turboshaft engines producing 4380 shp each
Length 30.3 metres **Height** 8.64 metres **Rotor diameter** 24.07 metres
Speed 150 knots
Maximum takeoff weight Internal load: 69,750 pounds (31,666 kilograms) External load: 73,500 pounds (33,369 kilograms)
Range without refueling: 540 nautical miles; with aerial refueling: indefinite
Armament Two XM-218 .50 calibre machine guns
Crew 3

Notes
The heavy lift helicopter of the USMC, the CH-53E is compatible with most amphibious ships and is routinely deployed at sea. The helicopter is capable of lifting 16 tons (at sea level) and transporting the load 50 nautical miles and returning. A typical load would be a 16,000 pound M198 howitzer or a 26,000 pound Light Armoured Vehicle. The aircraft also can retrieve downed aircraft including another CH-53E. The aircraft is equipped with a refuelling probe and can be refuelled in flight giving the helicopter virtually unlimited endurance. It is to be replaced in service by a new-build derivative, the CH-53K. The CH-53K will maintain virtually the same footprint (ie take up a similar deck space) as the CH-53E, but will nearly double the payload to 27,000 pounds over 110 nautical miles under "hot high" ambient conditions. The CH-53K's maximum gross weight will increase to 84,700 pounds versus 73,000 pounds for the CH-53E. Up to 156 aircraft could be acquired to replace roughly an equal number of CH-53Es.

US NAVY/PH2 MICHAEL J. SANDBERG

Sikorsky MH-53 SEA DRAGON

Variant MH-53E
Role Mine-countermeasures
Engines Three GE T64-GE-419 turboshaft engines (4,750 shp each)
Length Fuselage 22 metres; Overall 30.2 metres
Height 8.6 metres
Rotor Diameter 24.1 metres
Weight Max. Gross weight, w/external load: 69,750 lbs (31,693 kg); Max. Gross weight, w/internal load: 69,750 lb (31,693 kg); Empty weight 36,745 lb (16,667 kg)
Airspeed 150 knots **Ceiling** 10,000 feet.
Range Max: 1050 nautical miles.
Crew Two pilots, one to six aircrewmen
Load 55 troops or 32,000 pounds (14,512 kg) cargo

Notes

The MH-53E is heavier and has a greater fuel capacity than the Sea Stallion. Capable of transporting up to 55 troops, the MH-53E can carry a 16-ton payload 50 nautical miles, or a 10- ton payload 500 nautical miles. In its primary mission of airborne mine countermeasures, the helicopter is capable of towing a variety of mine-countermeasures systems. Aircraft assigned to HC-4 were modified with extra armour, fitted with a ramp mounted GAU-21 gun and night vision compatible cockpit lighting. Half of the squadron deployed to Iraq in 2006 to assist the hardworked CH-53 Sea Stallion.

Bell UH-1 IROQUOIS

Variants UH-1N; HH-1N
Role Assault; Medevac; Utility
Engines Two Pratt and Whitney T400-CP-400 turboshaft engines; 1,250 hp
Length 17 metres **Height** 4.4 metres **Rotor Diameter** 14.6 metres rotors spread
Weight Empty: 6,000 pounds (2,721.5 kg); Max Takeoff Weight: 10,500 pounds
(4,762.7 kg).
Airspeed 110 kts **Ceiling** 17,300 feet **Range** 286 miles
Armament M-240 7.62mm MG or GAU-16 .50 calibre MG or the GAU-17 7.62mm
automatic gun. All three weapons systems are crew-served, and the GAU-2B/A can
also be controlled by the pilot in the fixed forward firing mode. The helicopter can also
carry two 7-shot or 19-shot 2.75-inch rocket pods.
Crew Pilot, co-pilot, crew chief, gunner, plus 6 to 8 combat-equipped troops

Notes

First flown in the 1950's, the venerable "Huey" still gives sterling service today. In
USMC service the UH-1N can be deployed in command and control, resupply, casual-
ty evacuation, liaison and troop transport roles. The aircraft can be equipped with a
specialized communication package (ASC-26) for the command and control role and
in the medical evacuation role up to six stretcher patients and one medical attendant
can be accommodated. The HH-1N Iroquois helicopter is used by the USN for shore-
based search and rescue duties. An upgrade programme to provide 100 UH-1Y aircraft
is underway, featuring a new four-blade, composite rotor system, new transmission,
undercarriage and state-of-the-art cockpit. The upgrade will provide a dramatic
increase in range, speed and payload. The UH-1Y is expected to achieve full operational capability in 2012.

Bell AH-1 SUPER COBRA

Variants AH-1W
Role Attack helicopter
Engines Two General Electric T700-GE-401 engines
Length 17.67 metres **Height** 4.17 metres **Rotor Diameter** 14.62 metres
Speed 147 knots
Maximum takeoff weight 14,750 pounds (6,696.50 kilograms)
Range 256 nautical miles
Ceiling 18,700 feet (5703.5 metres) (limited to 10,000 feet by oxygen requirements)
Armament One 20MM turreted cannon with 750 rounds; four external wing stations that can fire 2.75-inch or 5-inch rockets and a wide variety of precision guided missiles, to include TOW/Hellfire (point target/anti-armour), Sidewinder (anti-air) Sidearm (anti-radar)
Crew 2

Notes
A day/night marginal weather USMC attack helicopter the AH-1W provides enroute escort for assault helicopters and their embarked forces. The AH-1W is a two-place, tandem-seat, twin-engine helicopter capable of land or sea based operations. It can provide fire support and fire support coordination to the landing force during amphibious assaults and subsequent operations ashore. The AH-1W is operated in eight composite HMLA squadrons composed of 18 AH-1 and 9 UH-1 aircraft. The AH-1W is constantly being upgraded, the latest variant including Night Targeting System/Forward Looking Infrared Radar to provide laser rangefinding/designating and camera capabilities. As with the UH-1, this helicopter is also undergoing an upgrade. 180 AH-1Z helicopters, featuring the same upgrades as the UH-1Y will reach full operational capability in 2018. The programme will achieve 84% commonality between the two aircraft types.

Bell-Boeing MV-22 OSPREY

Variants MV-22B
Role Assault transport for troops, equipment and supplies
Engines Two pivoting Rolls-Royce/Allison AE1107C engines
Rotor Diameter 11.58 metres **Blades per rotor** Three
Weight 60,500 lbs max
Airspeed 272 knots   **Ceiling** 25,000 feet
Crew 3 **Capacity** 24 troops

Notes

After many years in development, this unique tilt rotor is now entering service. The Osprey completed its final operational evaluation (OPEVAL) in June 2005. The MV-22 is capable of carrying 24 combat-equipped Marines or a 10,000-pound external load, and has a strategic self-deployment capability of 2,100 nautical miles with a single aerial refuelling. It is superior to the CH-46E it replaces - twice the speed, three times the payload, and six times the range. On 3 June 2006 the USMC helicopter squadron, HMM-263, was stood down to begin the process of upgrading to the MV-22 Osprey. HMM-263 was re-designated VMM-263, and reactivated on 3 March 2006 as the first MV-22 squadron. VMM-162 followed in 2006 and VMM-266 will be formed in 2007. Training is carried out by VMMT-204. On 28 September 2005, the Pentagon formally approved full-rate production for the Osprey. Planned production quantities include 360 aircraft for the USMC and 48 for the USN, with production at 24-48 aircraft a year. The aircraft can operate from all of the USNs big flat tops.

US NAVY/PH1 JOHN COLLINS

Lockheed P-3 ORION

Variants P-3C; EP-3E
Role ASW; Maritime Patrol; Recce and Intelligence collection
Engines Four Allison T-56-A-14 turboprop engines (4,900 shaft horsepower each)
Length 35.57 metres **Height** 10.27 metres **Wingspan** 30.36 metres
Weight Max gross take-off: 139,760 pounds (63,394.1 kg)
Airspeed maximum - 411 knots; cruise - 328 knots **Ceiling** 28,300 feet
Range Maximum mission range - 2,380 nautical miles; for three hours on station at 1,500 feet - 1,346 nautical miles
Crew 11 (22 EP-3E)
Armament 20,000 pounds (9 metric tons) of ordnance including: Harpoon (AGM-84D) cruise missiles, SLAM (AGM-84E) missiles, Maverick (AGM 65) air-to-ground missiles, MK-46/50 torpedoes, rockets, mines, depth bombs, and special weapons.

Notes

Originally designed as a land-based, long-range, anti-submarine warfare (ASW) patrol aircraft, the P-3C's mission has evolved to include surveillance of the battlespace, either at sea or over land. Its long range and long loiter time have proved invaluable assets. The EP-3E provides fleet and theatre commanders worldwide with near real-time tactical SIGINT. With sensitive receivers and high-gain dish antennas, the EP-3E is able to exploit a wide range of electronic emissions from deep within targeted territory.

The P-3C, which has reached the end of its service life, will be replaced by the P-8A Multi-mission Maritime Aircraft (MMA) which is based on the commercial Boeing 737 twin jet airframe. The P-8A programme completed a successful Preliminary Design Review in November 2005 and is working toward Critical Design Review planned for early 2007. A series of upgrades and inspections have been instigated to sustain the P-3C fleet as an effective force until the planned introduction of the P-8A in 2013.

Boeing E-6 MERCURY

Variant E-6B
Role Airborne Command Post
Engines Four CFM-56-2A-2 high bypass turbofan engines
Length 45.8 metres **Height** 12.9 metres **Wingspan** 45.2 metres
Weight Max. Gross, take-off: 341,000 lbs (153,900 kg)
Airspeed Approximately 522 knots
Ceiling 40,000+ feet **Range** 6,600 nautical miles
Crew 23

Notes

The E-6 Mercury aircraft was originally designed for the TACAMO (Take Charge and Move Out) role, providing emergency command and control of fleet ballistic missile submarines. The upgraded E-6B has now expanded its role to include that of Airborne Command Post being able to take on the role of the USAF's EC-135 aircraft, thus becoming a true dual mission aircraft. The planes provide a survivable communications link between national decision makers and the USA's arsenal of strategic nuclear weapons. It enables the President of the United States and the Secretary of Defence to directly contact submarines, bombers and missile silos.

US NAVY/MCS3 NATHAN LAIRD

Grumman C-2 GREYHOUND

Variant C-2A
Role Carrier On-board Delivery (COD) aircraft
Engines Two Allison T56-A-425 turboprop engines; 4,600 shp each
Length 17.3 metres **Height** 5.28 metres **Wingspan** 24.56 metres
Weight Max. Gross, take-off: 57,500 lbs (26,082 kg)
Airspeed Cruise - Approximately 260 kts; Max - Approximately 343 kts
Ceiling 30,000 feet **Range** 1,300 nautical miles
Crew Four

Notes

A derivative of the E-2 Hawkeye, the Greyhound provides critical logistics support to Carrier Strike Groups. Its primary mission is the transport of high-priority cargo, mail and passengers between carriers and shore bases. It can deliver a combined payload of 10,000 pounds over a distance in excess of 1,000 nm. The interior arrangement of the cabin can readily accommodate cargo, passengers and stretcher cases. Priority cargo such as jet engines can be transported from shore to ship in a matter of hours. A cargo cage system or transport stand provides restraint for loads during launches and landings. The large aft cargo ramp/door and a powered winch allow straight-in rear cargo loading and unloading for fast turnaround. The C-2A's in-flight ramp open capability allows for the airdrop of supplies and personnel.

US NAVY/PH2 DANIEL J. McLAIN

Boeing C-9 SKYTRAIN II

Variants C-9A/B/C
Role Aeromedical evacuation, C-9B cargo transport
Engines Two Pratt & Whitney JT8D-9A turbofans
Length 35.7 metres **Height** 8.2 metres **Wingspan** 27.9 metres
Weight 65,283 pounds (29,369 kg) in passenger configuration; 59,706 pounds
(26,868 kg) in cargo configuration; Maximum takeoff weight is 108,000 pounds
(48,600 kg)
Airspeed 565 mph at 25,000 feet with maximum takeoff weight
Ceiling 37,000 feet
Range 2,000+ miles
Crew C-9A/C, eight (pilot, copilot, flight mechanic, two flight nurses, three aeromedical
technicians); C-9B, two pilots plus cabin attendants
Load 40 stretcher patients or four stretchers and 40 ambulatory patients or other
combinations

Notes

The C-9 fleet is located throughout the continental United States, Europe, and Asia.
The USN and USMC C-9 aircraft provide cargo and passenger transportation as well
as forward deployment logistics support.

Boeing C-40 CLIPPER

Variants C-40A
Role Logistics Support
Engines Two CFM56-7 SLST turbofans
Length 33.63 metres **Height** 12.55 metres **Wingspan** 34.3 metres
Weight Maximum takeoff weight is 171,000 pounds
Airspeed 585 - 615mph **Ceiling** 41,000 feet
Range 3,000+ nm with 121 passengers or 40,000 lbs of cargo
Crew Four

Notes

The C-40A Clipper is a derivative of the Boeing 737 commercial airliner and has been procured to replace the ageing C-9B/DC-9 Skytrain II. Operated by the USN Reserve these aircraft provide critical logistics support to the USN. The USN purchased nine C-40A aircraft using a Commercial Off the Shelf (COTS) strategy. The first aircraft was delivered in April 2001.

The USN operates smaller utility logistics aircraft, including the C-12 Huron for short haul cargo transfer and VIP/Passenger transport operations. C-20/C-37 Gufstream aircraft have been procured to operate in the executive transport role and will replace the remaining VP-3 Orion, which has been operating on a waiver.

Lockheed C-130 HERCULES

Variants C-130T; KC-130F/R/T; KC-130J
Role Global airlift and inflight refuelling
Propulsion Four Allison T56-A-15 turboprops, each 4,300 horsepower
Length 29.3 metres   **Height** 11.4 metres   **Wingspan** 39.7 metres
Weight Maximum takeoff weight 155,000 pounds (69,750 kg)
Airspeed 374 mph at 20,000 feet
Ceiling 33,000 feet with 100,000 pounds (45,000 kg) payload
Range 2,050 nautical miles with max payload; 2,174 nautical miles with 25,000 pounds (11,250 kg) cargo; 4,522 nautical miles with no cargo
Crew Five: two pilots, navigator, flight engineer, loadmaster
Load Up to 92 troops or 64 paratroops or 74 stretcher patients or five standard freight pallets

Notes

Used by the USN in a variety of roles from transport and logistics support to launching aerial target drones. The USMC KC-130 is a multi-role, multi-mission tactical tanker/transport which provides the support required by Marine Air Ground Task Forces. This versatile aircraft provides in-flight refuelling to both tactical aircraft and helicopters as well as rapid ground refuelling when required. The latest variant of the aircraft, the KC-130J offers increases in speed, altitude, range and performance. It can be configured for cargo missions without losing the ability to conduct air refuelling, or, if the mission dictates, it can be configured exclusively for refuelling by adding an internal fuel tank. Additionally, the KC-130J can be used as a platform for the establishment of a Forward Arming and Refuelling Point (FARP). The KC-130J provides increased reliability, capability and mission flexibility with its satellite communications system, survivability enhancements, night systems, and enhanced aircraft systems.

Lockheed T-2 BUCKEYE

Variants T-2C
Role All-purpose jet trainer
Engines Two General Electric 085-GE-4 turbojets (2,950 lbs thrust each)
Length 11 metres   **Height** 4.7 metres   **Wingspan** 10.3 metres
Weight Take-off max. 13,180 pounds (5,931 kg); empty 8,115 pounds (3,652 kg)
Airspeed 521 mph
Ceiling 44,400 feet
Range 910 miles
Armament Provision for gun pods, bombs or rockets under wings
Crew Two (instructor and student pilot)

Notes

The T-2 is a two-seat trainer used to train pilots and flight officers in basic and intermediate strike training. It entered service in 1968 and is gradually being replaced by the T-45C Goshawk.

Boeing T-45 GOSHAWK

Variants T-45A/C
Role Training platform for Navy/Marine Corps pilots
Engine Rolls Royce F405-RR-401 turbofan engine with 5,527 pounds thrust
Length 11.98 metres   **Height** 4.11 metres   **Wingspan** 9.39 metres
Weight Take-off maximum gross, 13,500 pounds (6,075 kg); empty 9,394 pounds (4,261 kg)
Airspeed 645 mph   **Ceiling** 42,500 feet
Range 700 nautical miles (805 statute miles, 1288 km)
Crew Two (instructor and student pilot)
Armament None

Notes

Developed from the very successful British Hawk trainer, the T-45 Goshawk is a carrier-capable trainer aircraft which is gradually replacing the T-2C Buckeye and TA–4J Skyhawk as the Navy's strike trainer. The T-45A, which became operational in 1991, contains an analogue design cockpit while the new T-45C (began delivery in December 1997) is built around a new digital "glass cockpit" design. The USN has 187 T-45s in service.

North American Rockwell T-39 SABRELINER

Variants T-39G/N
Role Twin jet and Navigation trainer
Engine Two Pratt & Whitney J-60-P-3 engines; 3,000lb thrust each
Length 13.41 metres   **Height** 4.88 metres   **Wingspan** 13.56 metres
Weight Take-off maximum gross, 18,650 pounds (8,460 kg)
Airspeed 434 mph   **Ceiling** 42,000 feet
Range 1,476 nautical miles
Crew Two (7 students/passengers)
Armament None

Notes
The handful of T-39N Sabreliners remaining in service are used to train naval flight officers in radar navigation and airborne radar-intercept procedures.   These aircraft
replaced the Cessna T-47A during the early 1990s. Eight T-39Gs are used for student
non-radar training. The U.S. Air Force's T-1A Jayhawk is used interchangeably with the
T-39 Sabreliner for advanced naval flight officer/navigator training at NAS Pensacola.

A further twin engined turbo-prop trainer, the Raytheon T-44A Pegasus (operated by
VT-31 Wise Owls), is used for advanced turboprop aircraft training and for intermediate E2/C2 (carrier based turboprop radar aircraft) training at the Naval Air Station,
Corpus Christi, Texas. The T-44 is equipped with deicing and anti-icing systems augmented by instrumentation and navigation equipment which allows flight under instrument and icing conditions. A number of C-12 Huron aircraft have been converted to be
used in the trainer role as TC-12s (operated by VT-35 Stingrays).

Raytheon T-6 TEXAN II

Variants T-6A
Role All-purpose turbo-prop trainer
Propulsion one Pratt & Whitney Canada PT-6A-68 turboprop engine; 1,100 hp
Length 10.12 metres **Height** 3.29 metres **Wingspan** 10.18 metres
Weight empty, 5,000 pounds (2,268 kg.); maximum takeoff weight, 6,500 pounds (2,948.4 kg)
Airspeed 270 knots at 1,000 feet level flight
Ceiling 31,000 feet
Range 900 nautical miles
Crew Two (instructor and student pilot)

Notes

The T-6A Texan II is a tandem-seat, turboprop trainer introduced in 2002 to train USN and USMC pilots. The aircraft is one component of the Joint Primary Aircraft Training System (JPATS) along with simulators, computeraided academics, and a Training Integration Management System (TIMS). The USN has a total requirement for 328 aircraft by 2017. They are replacing the T-34C.

Raytheon T-34 TURBO MENTOR

Variant T-34C
Role Training aircraft for Navy/Marine Corps pilots
Engine Model PT6A-25 turbo-prop engine (Pratt & Whitney Aircraft of Canada)
Length 9 metres **Height** 3 metres **Wingspan** 10 metres
Weight 4,425 lb, Empty Wt. approx. 3,000 lb
Airspeed Max: 280 Knots **Ceiling** 25,000 Feet **Range** Approximately 600 nautical miles
Crew Two (instructor and student pilot)

Notes

The T-34C is used to provide primary flight training for student pilots. As a secondary mission, approximately 10 percent of the aircraft provide pilot proficiency and other aircraft support services to Commander, Naval Air Force, U.S. Atlantic Fleet; Commander, Naval Air Force, U.S. Pacific Fleet; and Naval Air Systems Command's "satellite sites" operated throughout the continental United States. The T-34C was procured as a commercial-derivative aircraft certified under an FAA Type Certificate. The T-34C was derived from the civilian Beechcraft Bonanza. Throughout its life, the aircraft has been operated and commercially supported by the Navy using FAA processes, procedures and certifications.

Bell H-57 SEA RANGER

Variants TH-57B/C
Role Flying training
Engine One Allison 250-C20BJ turbofan engine
Length Fuselage - 9.44 metres; Rotors turning - 11.9 metres
Height 3.04 metres
Rotor Diameter 10.78 metres
Weight 1595 pounds (725kg) empty, 3200 pounds (1455 kg) maximum take off
Airspeed 138 mph; 117 mph cruising
Ceiling 18,900 feet
Range 368 nautical miles
Crew One pilot, four students

Notes

The TH-57 Sea Ranger is a derivative of the commercial Bell Jet Ranger 206 and is used to train several hundred student naval aviators with 45 TH-57Bs (for primary visual flight rules training) and 71 TH-57Cs (for advanced instrument flight rules training) in two helicopter training squadrons at NAS Whiting Field, Milton, Fla. Two TH-57Cs configured for RDT&E are used for photo, chase and utility missions at the Naval Air Warfare Center Aircraft Division at Patuxent River, Maryland.

McDD TH-6B CAYUSE

Variant TH-6B
Role Training Helicopter for US Naval Test Pilots School
Engine Allison T63-A-720 turbo shaft
Length 9.33 metres **Height** 2.3 metres
Weight 2,550 lb, Empty Wt. approx. 1,138 lb
Airspeed Max: 130 Knots **Ceiling** 15,000+ Feet **Range** 300 nautical miles
Crew Two (instructor and student pilot)

Notes

The TH-6B is the Navy derivative of the MD-369H. The TH-6B is an integral part of the United States Naval Test Pilot School's test pilot training syllabus. The aircraft and associated instrumentation and avionics are used for the in-flight instruction and demonstration of flying qualities, performance and mission systems flight test techniques.

Northrop Grumman F-5 TIGER

Variant F-5N (single seat); F-5F (twin seat)
Role Simulated Air-to-Air Combat Training
Engine Two J85-GE-21C turbojet engines; 5,000 pounds (2,273 kg) of thrust each
Length 14.4 metres **Height** 4.1 metres **Wingspan** 8.1 metres (figures for F-5N)
Weight 24,722 lb, Empty Wt. approx. 9,723 lb
Airspeed Max: Mach 1.64 **Ceiling** 50,000+ Feet
Range Approximately 2,314 nautical miles
Crew F-5N - One; F-5F - Two

Notes

The F-5N is a single seat, twin-engine, tactical fighter and attack aircraft providing simulated air-to-air combat training. Manufactured by Northrop Grumman Corporation the F-5F is a dual-seat version, twin-engine, tactical fighter commonly used for training and adversary combat tactics. The aircraft serves in an aggressor-training role with simulation capability of current threat aircraft in fighter combat mode.The USN also operate a number of early generation F-16A Fighting Falcons in the Aggressor role. These aircraft are primarily assigned to The Naval Strike and Air Warfare Centre (Top Gun) located at NAS Fallon, Nevada, with detachments at Key West, Florida and MCAS Yuma, Arizona

NAVY FLIGHT DEMONSTRATION SQUADRON
THE BLUE ANGELS

At the end of World War II, Admiral Chester W. Nimitz, the Chief of Naval Operations, ordered the formation of a flight demonstration team to keep the public interested in Naval Aviation. The Blue Angels performed their first flight demonstration less than a year later in June 1946 at their home base, Naval Air Station (NAS) Jacksonville, Florida. Flying the Grumman F6F Hellcat, they were led by Lt. Cmdr. Roy "Butch" Voris. Only two months later on 25 August 1946, the Blue Angels transitioned to the Grumman F8F Bearcat and introduced the famous "diamond" formation.

Throughout the 1950s and 60s the team transitioned to various jet aircraft and built a reputation for very close, tight formation flying. In 1974 the team was re-organised into a Squadron and began flying the Skyhawk. In 1986 the team adopted the F/A-18 as its display aircraft and continues to thrill airshow crowds around the world. The six blue and gold aircraft are supported by a similarly coloured C-130T from the USMC, affectionately known as "Fat Albert". In addition to the aircraft's support and logistics role, she also takes part in the flying programme, a highlight of which is a rocket assisted take-off.

Details of the Squadrons annual display schedules can be found on their website:

www.blueangels.navy.mil

COMMAND EXCELLENCE AWARDS

The bridge wings of many USN ships proudly boast colourful displays of letters, which to the layman can be quite baffling, but to the sailors themselves are a proud display of their accomplishments. Known as Command Excellence Awards, each letter means that the ship wearing them has proven itself to be superior in specific fields of operation. The colour and letter combinations denote different departments within the ship. However, the award which most crews strive for is the Battle E. Whereas all the other awards may be awarded to all crews, there is only one Battle E awarded per squadron each year. The ship awarded the Battle E has proven itself across all departments and across all warfare disciplines. The Battle E is displayed larger than the other awards and is shadowed in appearance (see bottom right of picture below).

Awards are only valid for one year after which they must be removed, or regained. The retention of an award for a consecutive year is indicated with a diagonal strip below the letter. If the ship wins the award for five consecutive years, the letter is displayed with a star above it, replacing the stripes. In the case of the coveted Battle E, five consecutive years is displayed by a gold E with a silver star above. Further five year periods are marked by additional stars.

Sailors from the cruiser USS CHANCELLORSVILLE show off their display of awards which include a gold "Battle E". Propulsion and Engineering; Supply; Air and Maritime Warfare have all been awarded Command Excellence Awards - the Supply Department receiving the award over ten consecutive years!

COMMAND EXCELLENCE AWARDS

E   Award for the best seamanship, warfare drills, command and control, and preparedness to fulfill mission objectives. Only one award per squadron.

E   Best Propulsion and Engineering Department.

E   Best Combat Information Centre. (Surface Ships)

            Award for Operations Excellence. (Submarines)

E   Best Supply Departments.

E   Maritime Warfare Excellence. (Surface Ships)

            Aviation Maintenance Excellence. (Aircraft Carriers)

E   Best Air Department.

A   Award for Anti-submarine Warfare Excellence.

C   Excellence Award for the best Communication Departments.

CS   Award for Combat Systems Excellence on board the Aircraft Carriers.

D   Excellence Award for the best Deck Departments.

D   Dental Award.

DC   Excellence Award for the best Damage Control Crews.

F   Award for Fire Control Excellence.

H   Wellness Award for the best Health Promotion Activities. Units have to apply for this award.

H   Habitability Award.

M or M   Best Medical Departments.

N or N   Award for Navigation Excellence.

R   Award for Repair Excellence.

T   Award for Tactical Proficiency.

W   Best Weapons Departments on board an Aircraft Carrier.

            Navigation Award (Represented by a white ship's wheel)

            Deck Seamanship Award (Represented by white crossed anchors).

GLOSSARY

The military throughout the world have a passion for acronyms and abbreviations - and the US Armed Forces are no exception. Any modern day reference book will be liberally scattered with these, sometimes annoying, abbreviations - second nature to those in the know, but frustrating for the general reader. The following pages should help you through some of the 'alphabet soup' that will inevitably be found in this volume.

AAG	Advanced Arresting Gear	EMALS	Electro Magnetic Aircraft Launch System
ABM	Anti-ballistic Missile		
ADCAP	Advanced Capability	EMNS	Expendable Mine Neutralization System
AEM/S	Advanced Enclosed Mast/Sensor		
		ESG	Expeditionary Strike Group
ARG	Amphibious Ready Group		
ARS	Auxiliary Rescue and Salvage Vessel	ESSM	Evolved Sea Sparrow Missile
AS	Submarine Depot Ship	EW	Electronic Warfare
ASROC	Anti-submarine Rocket	FFG	Frigate (Guided Missile)
ASW	Anti-submarine Warfare	FL	Full Load
CEC	Co-operative Engagement Capability	FRP	Fleet Response Plan
		FSF	Fast Sea Frame
C4ISR	Command, Control, Communicaions, Computers, Intelligence, Surveillance and Reconnaissance	FSS	Fast Sealift Ship
		GD	General Dynamics
		GE	General Electric
		GTS	Gas Turbine Ship
		HM	Helicopter Mine Countermeasures Squadron
CG	Cruiser		
CG(X)	Cruiser (Next Generation)		
CIWS	Close In Weapon System	HMH	USMC Heavy Helicopter Squadron
COTS	Commercial Off The Shelf		
CSG	Carrier Strike Group	HMLA	USMC Light Attack Helicopter Squadron
CVBG	Carrier Battle Group		
CV	Aircraft Carrier	HMM	USMC Medium Helicopter Squadron
CVN	Aircraft Carrier (Nuclear)		
CVW	Carrier Air Wing	HMMT	USMC Heavy Helicopter Training Squadron
DDG	Destroyer (Guided Missile)		
		HMT	USMC Helicopter Training Squadron
DSRV	Deep Submergence Recovery Vehicle		
		HSC	Helicopter Sea Combat Squadron
EB	General Dynamics (Electric Boat)		
		HSM	Helicopter Maritime Strike Squadron
EFV	Expeditionary Fighting Vehicle		
		HSV	High Speed Vessel

HT	Helicopter Training Squadron	MG	Machine Gun
IBU	Inshore Boat Unit	MHC	Coastal Minesweeper
ICBM	Inter Continental Ballistic Missile	MIRV	Multiple Independently Targeted Re-entry Vehicles
JPATS	Joint Primary Air Training System	MLE	Mission Life Extension
LASH	Lighter Aboard Ship	MMA	Multi-mission Maritime Aircraft
LCAC	Landing Craft (Air Cushion)	MPF	Maritime Pre-positioning Force
LCC	Amphibious Command and Control Ship	MPF(F)	Maritime Pre-positioning Force (Future)
LCS	Littoral Combat Ship	MPS	Maritime Pre-positioning Squadron
LCU	Landing Craft (Utility)		
LFA	Low Frequency Array	MSC	Military Sealift Command
LHA	Landing Ship, Helicopter Assault	MT	Motor Tanker
		MV	Merchant Vessel
LHA(R)	Landing Ship, Helicopter Assault (Replacement)	NAB	Naval Amphibious Base
		NAS	Naval Air Station
LHD	Landing Ship Helicopter, Dock	NAVSEA	Naval Sea Systems Command
LKA	Landing Ship, Attack, Cargo	NAWC	Naval Air Warfare Centre
		NCWRON	Naval Coastal Warfare Squadron
LM	Lockheed Martin		
LMSR	Large, Medium Speed Ro-Ro	NDRF	National Defence Reserve Force
LPD	Landing Ship, Personnel, Dock	NFAF	Naval Fleet Auxiliary Force
LSD	Landing Ship, Dock	NGNN	Northrop Gruman Newport News
LST	Landing Ship, Tank		
LSV	Large Scale Vessel	NGSS	Northrop Grumman Ship Systems
MARAD	Maritime Administration		
MAW	USMC Air Wing	OPDS	Offshore Petroleum Distribution System
MCAS	Marine Corps Air Station		
MCDS	Modular Cargo Delivery Syetem	OPEVAL	Operational Evaluation
		PC	Patrol Craft
MCM	Mine Countermeasures Vessel	PPIP	Planned Product Improvement Programme
MCS	Mine Warfare Command and Support Vessel	RAM	Rolling Airframe Missile
		RO-RO	Roll On - Roll Off
MEF	Marine Expeditionary Force	RRF	Ready Reserve Fleet
		SALM	Single Anchor Leg Moor

SB	Shipbuilder	T-AOT	Auxiliary Transport Tanker
SEAL	Sea Air and Land (USN Special Forces)	T-AOE	Auxiliary Fast Combat Support Ship
SLEP	Service Life Extension Programme	T-ARC	Auxiliary Cable Repair Ship
SS	Steam Ship	T-AVB	Auxiliary Aviation Logistics Ship
SSN	Attack Submarine (Nuclear Powered)	T-ARS	Auxiliary Rescue and Salvage Ship
SSBN	Ballistic Missile Submarine (Nuclear Powered)	T-ATF	Auxiliary Fleet Tug
		USCG	US Coast Guard
		USMC	US Marine Corps
SSGN	Cruise Missile Submarine (Nuclear Powered)	USNS	United States Naval Ship
		USS	United States Ship
SSV	Submarine Support Vessel	VAW	Airborne Early Warning Squadron
SURTASS	Surface Towed Array System	VAQ	Electronic Warfare Squadron
SWATH	Small Waterplane Twin Hull	VFA	Fighter Attack Squadron
SY	Shipyard	VLS	Vertical Launch System
TACAMO	Take Charge & Move Out	VMA	USMC Attack Squadron
TACTOM	Tactical Tomahawk	VMAQ	USMC Electronic Warfare Squadron
T-ACS	Auxiliary Crane Ship		
T-AE	Auxiliary Ammunition Ship	VMFA	USMC Fighter Attack Squadron
T-AFS	Auxiliary Combat Stores Ship	VMFA(AW)	USMC Fighter Attack Squadron (All Weather)
T-AGF	Auxiliary Command Ship	VMFT	USMC Fighter Training Squadron
T-AGM	Auxiliary Range Instrumentation Ship	VMGR	USMC Tanker/Transport Squadron
T-AGOR	Auxiliary Acoustic Survey Ship	VMM	USMC Tilt Rotor Squadron
T-AGOS	Auxiliary Ocean Surveillance Ship	VP	Maritime Patrol Squadron
		VQ	Special Warfare Squadron
T-AGS	Auxiliary Oceonographic Survey Ship	VR	Transport Squadron
		VRC	Composite Transport Squadron
T-AH	Auxiliary Hospital Ship		
T-AKE	Auxiliary Dry Cargo Ship	VS	Anti-Submarine Squadron
T-AK	Auxiliary Transport, Container	V/STOL	Vertical/Short Take-off or Landing
T-AKR	Auxiliary Transport, Ro-Ro		
T-AO	Auxiliary Fleet Replenishment Oiler	VT	Training Squadron
		VX	Trials Squadron